EDITOR

C000061448

MONIZA ALVI & ESTHER

We are most comfortable being hidden but we yearn to be seen.
– Jane Hirshfield, quoted in 'Work in Progress' by Linda France

O n an ordinary March day in 2011, staff at the Scottish Poetry Library were amazed to discover an exquisite sculpture carved from paper left anonymously on a table in the library, with a message in support of "libraries, books, words, ideas". This was the first in a series of sculptures which appeared over the next few months at a variety of book-related venues around Edinburgh, each one greeted with excitement and delight. When we were approached to be guest editors of *Poetry Review* we agreed that we'd love our edition to engender something of the same spirit of generous play. And so the idea of the Anonymous Invitation was born: a plan to approach a number of established poets to ask them to contribute a poem anonymously and to reflect on the experience.

While this might seem a light-hearted exercise, we hope it goes some way to rehabilitating the idea of anonymity. Hardly a week goes by without a story which gives Anon, as it were, a bad name. Whether it's hacking, cyber-bullying or mindless trolling, anonymity in the digital age seems to offer the means of masking our worst instincts. What the paper sculpture artist reminded us is that the freedom anonymity brings can be a creative as well as a destructive space.

We were particularly interested in whether this is how it would strike our invited poets. While it's never been so easy to be nameless, it's also never been so difficult to be private. Many poets are still working out their relationship with social media and how to navigate a world of instant communication which is at odds with the inward-dwelling, time-taking nature of writing poems. We wanted to offer writers whom we admire the truly blank page of an anonymous submission – a space outside the Web with its intricate (and sometimes sticky) threads of reputation and expectation.

We're also eager to hear how readers find the experience of encountering poems shorn of biographical context. In her compelling 'micro essays' in our Centrefold section, Jen Hadfield talks about the "courtesies" of the interaction between poet and reader and the creation of meaning as a collaborative act. Perhaps that becomes easier when a poem is un-attributed. The popular reception of an artist like Banksy, who occupies the curiously contemporary space of being simultaneously unknown and world famous, suggests a hunger for imaginative anonymity. Partly curiosity driven, yes, but also surely a response to the artist's gift, the sudden appearance of something beautiful and thought-provoking, like a birthday present on a day you weren't born.

Jen's piece also recognises the dangers inherent in publication and the difficulties of discovering and then maintaining "the uninhibited voice". The risk of recognition, of being named, certainly has a resonance when we consider the history of women's poetry and its reception. Our anonymously written poems prompt us to contemplate the gender of their authors – and may well lead us to the larger question of what constitutes women's poetry, or poetries, today. To help us take stock of the current landscape, and to celebrate the twentieth anniversary of the ground-breaking anthology *Sixty Women Poets*, we invited its editor, Linda France, to contribute an essay reflecting on where we are now in terms of women's poetry. We are keen also to consider men's poetry in the context of gender shifts, and, with this in mind, we asked Tim Liardet to bring a personal perspective to bear on poetry and masculinity.

In her essay, Linda France talks about the need for positive discrimination in publishing women's poetry at the time of *Sixty Women Poets*. It's a sign of progress, perhaps, that we didn't feel the same obligation in our role as editors of *Poetry Review*, though it is the case that poems by women are in the majority in our edition. This, however, reflects the submissions ratio – there was a very strong postbag which included many intriguing poems by women. We were on the look-out for poems which demanded our attention and conveyed a sense of urgency in the writing. Those we've selected also seem to us to have a haunting quality, and often present alternative worlds, whether cultural or imaginative. Our Reviews section is more actively gendered than our main Poetry section in that we wanted to give prominence to fine women reviewers, reviewing books by men as well as women. Many books are discussed (by men as well as by women) including those on this year's woman-strong T.S. Eliot shortlist.

Women have often gained from the experience of working collaboratively, as in the poetry workshops explored in Jackie Wills's article – workshops that have played such a crucial part in the empowerment of those who are not "male, white and middle-class", or have considered themselves outsiders. Our editorial process was a collaborative one and we were pleased to develop our ideas jointly and to exchange views. We are grateful to the Poetry Society for its flexibility in enabling us to work together – a 'job-sharing' that we found helpful both practically and creatively.

Finally, we are glad to include John Greening's tribute to Dennis O'Driscoll who died on Christmas Eve. The sense of poetry comradeship, of connection, was fostered uniquely by Dennis whose astute, humane poetry spoke so memorably to readers and listeners.

Contents

Volume 103:1 Spring 2013

CENTREFOLD

REVIEWS

POEMS

ℬ

It's midnight butterfly it's now or never.

– *Valérie Rouzeau*

Sarah Roby
Ritual

Secular living still needs ritual
– the gathering of us through thicks and thins,
people-deep around a new arrival
or the touch – just – of hands in grieving.
Patterns like these can soothe and form,
from templates pressed into the air,
a horse-shoe, love-heart or key-to-the-door
that make the invisible almost there.

And each one with its quirk of accuracy
is like a morning climb up the stairs
taking half a cup of tea exactly
in a gesture of some red ruby years;
or the faithful precision of a weekly row,
a reminder that we matter, here, now.

D.M. Black
The Arrow-Maker

The arrow-maker has beautiful hands: they are strong and slender.
He glues the flight to the shank with unpausing, definite movements.
With his steady gaze before him, he weighs the arrowheads in his hand –
He makes a decision, he binds one head to the shaft,
Winding the tough thread round, again and again, correcting for overlaps;
Then glues the thread in its place, then varnishes the length of the arrow –
Then stands it to dry out of sight, in the deep shade in back of the door-light.

But the arrow-maker is young: he would like to be out with his mates catching
                                                                squirrels
Or gambling for beans in the village, with breaks for philosophising and
                                                                horse-play.
Or perhaps going off with a girl, past the small fields into the forest
To which they are called by the Meaning of Life, dreaming and loving...
Or he would like to be down at the river, admiring its wrestling currents
Or dizzy seeing its broad, shining floor, forever in decorous motion.

It is a burden for the arrow-maker that he has to make arrows, that his people
                                                                depend on him.
He sits in the doorway in sunlight, not looking up from his task
Or looking up when someone approaches, and calling out to them cheerfully.
He is identified with his task: you couldn't say he is sorrowful
Or that he's proud, exactly, to have this use for his dark eyes and beautiful hands.

Mara Bergman
The Tailor's Three Sons

Nights I can't sleep, I think about the tailor's
three sons and how twelve people lived and worked
in a three-room apartment meant for four when
the Lower East Side was the most crowded place

on the planet. What was it they did? The cutting or basting
or sewing, right here, the finishing or pressing over there
while the clock's heavy ticking kept them sane, insane?
Afternoons they'd elbow through the teeming streets to catch

some air, some news, but after a long day, what else had they
to look forward to but a bowl of soup and then to sleep
on the red velvet sofa which looked, from a distance,
more lavish, and though cherished, was so narrow

it is hard to imagine enough room for even one young boy
to sit down. I think of the sons because when night came
at last, and the whirr of machines had flown out the window,
the clock's ticking rocking like a lullaby, they would

lay down their heads side by side on the sofa,
rest their throbbing feet on wooden chairs and lie, suspended,
to sleep the sleep of the young and the exhausted,
dreaming their immigrant dreams in thin air.

David Morley
The Invisible Gift

John Clare weaves English words into a nest
and in the cup he stipples rhyme, like mud,
to clutch the shape of something he can hold
but not yet hear; and in the hollow of his hearing,
he feathers a space with a down of verbs
and nouns heads-up. There. Clare lays it down
and nestles over its forming sound: taps and lilts,
the steady knocking of the nib on his hand until
it hatches softly beneath him. And when he peers
below his palm, he spies its eyes, hears its peeps,
but does not know what to think. He strokes
its tottering yolk-wet crown; feels a nip against
his thumb, buds of muscle springy at the wing, and all
the hungers of the world to come for this small singing.

Nicola Warwick
Mary Shelley's Version

Last night, I dreamt your touch
gave me a baby; hand to hand
we were, no more
than a subtle brush of palms.

Because no one knew,
I birthed our baby
in my pocket to keep it safe.

Because no one knew,
I suffered the ache
of not being able to mother,
couldn't rush to give it milk
whenever it cried.

Because no one knew,
we couldn't tell anyone
when our baby died,
nor revive it no matter how
we rubbed and rubbed its chest
before the fire.

Cheryl Moskowitz
Fanny Burney Undergoes A Mastectomy, 30 September 1811

Source: Fanny Burney Selected Letters and Journals, *ed. Joyce Hemlow (OUP, 1986)*

At 10 o'clock he said he would be with me. I sent word that I could not be
ready till one.
I finished my breakfast, though not with much appetite, you will understand.

I had a bed, and Curtains and Heaven knows what else to get ready. Obliged
to quit my room twice to put it in order. Still this business was good for
my nerves.

When all was ready the Coast was clear but this indeed was a dreadful interval.
I had only to think, and you alone can know that time spent thus is
never-ending.

The sight of bandages, sponges, Lint made me a little sick. I walked forwards
and back until I quieted all emotion and became, by degrees, without sentiment

or consciousness. And thus remained until the Clock struck three. A sudden
spirit of exertion returned. I took my pen, my right arm no longer worth sparing.

A few words I wrote for each of you while Carriages, one, two, three, four
followed one another, arriving in quick succession, and one Doctor came in to see

if I were alive. He gave me a wine cordial and left me speechless.
The Room was entered by seven Men in black and I could not utter a syllable.

Two old mattresses were demanded and an old Sheet. I began to tremble
violently, more with distaste and horror of the preparations than fear of the pain.

They desired me to mount the Bedstead but I stood suspended, wondering
to escape.
My maid was crying, the Nurses too. "Let all those women go!" my surgeon cried.

I said "No!" my Voice returned a little to its former animation. Oh how
did I long for my Sisters then? My Esther, my Charlotte – my departed Angel!

My distress, I suppose was apparent, though not my Wishes, for the men's hold did not lessen. "Can You," I cried, "feel for an operation that must seem so Trivial?"

"Yes it is a little thing," the surgeon stammered but could not go on. I myself softened
as I watched him grow more agitated. A glance showed me he was pale as ashes.

They placed me on the mattress, spread a Cambric handkerchief upon my face through which I could see the glitter of polished Steel. I closed my Eyes. Silence.

I did not breathe. The Doctor tried vainly to find any pulse. The pause broken at last by a voice of melancholy, unanswered. "Who will hold the centre?"

This arose me from my passive state. Somehow I knew they had found the whole breast infected.
Again the Cambric. Through it I watched a straight line described from top to bottom.

First a Cross, then a Circle. Yes the WHOLE was to be taken off. I started up, threw off my veil. "C'est moi, Monsieur!" I held my hand under it

and then resigned. You will rejoice my Dear, to hear that once resolved I needed no injunction not to restrain my cries and began a scream that lasted

the whole time of the incision. Steel on veins – arteries – flesh – nerves. The air that rushed to these parts was a mass of sharp, forked poniards.

Cutting against the grain alas my flesh resisted in a manner so forcible as to oppose and tire the hand of the operator. Yet still it was renewed.

I did not attempt to open my Eyes. Eyelids indented onto my Cheeks, the Doctor's hand rested but Oh Heaven! I could feel the knife tackling the bone.

I could not, dear Esther, not for days not for Weeks, speak of this business without again going through it. Even now, I am disordered by giving this account.

To conclude, the evil was profound though I bore it with all the courage I could exert.
I never moved, never stopped their faces from being streaked with my blood.

Angus Sinclair
Kertész At His Window

Shadows pass from roof to roof, long dark necks
extend from smokeless chimneys, distortions,
doubles, stackscapes fold over stoops and steps
or dart through windows into strangers' homes.

This is the view you are fixing. I watch
as your negative projection is thrown
out from your heels and dances up the wall.
Silhouette is not a language of tone

but of shape. Oh how our others rippled
impossibly down those *escaliers*!
foreshortened, elongated and coupled
by mood. They stood for something ill-expressed

by complex gradations of grey. *André,*
excuse me. Your shadow looks good today.

Judy Brown
After the Discovery of Linear Perspective

You gave us new places to hide. Arcades and piazzas are excavated
from your backgrounds in diptychs and altarpieces, just for the hell.
Some of our local heroes turn out to be smallish men. They whisper

to their spotted hounds whilst the eaves of their homes recede. Stairs
strut and coil like tempters behind the colour-coded Holy Family,
the bishops, the patrons, the endlessly-bystanding centurion. We all

toe the lines, the vanishing points, the black and white ostentation
of floors. Perhaps the molten paint matters more than what's painted –
this has become one of your tools, a closeted flourish of show and tell.

Yet I miss their warmth: the maidens and saints twisted to press
at the picture plane, all breathy frottage, and damp like flowers under glass.
Come, technician, let us brush past the samey glamours of Joseph

and Mary. Christ, there is so much gorgeous air explaining itself
in the back of your painting! Let's inhale its new space, shout
merely to gather echoes, make gestures that astonish us both.

Umami

With ginger tea, with steak on blue porcelain,
her husband's cooking plays my spicy tongue,
riffs on its various areas: salt, sweet, umami.
He chivvies us into sourness like a personal trainer –
serves Japanese since her doctor forbade chilli.

It is ginger we keep coming back to: the tingling
rhizome. Its pageant flowers drip in every vase
in their house. I brought ginger nuts from England.
She wanted hard biscuits against the chemo's nausea,
the kind she once crunched on cross-Channel ferries.

The terrace swarms with plants which none of us
were born to. The strength goes out of our bodies
in the conditioned air. The ceiling fans swallow
time – supercool and slow – but nothing
can stop the humidity from softening the biscuits.

While I play tourist, her fast cells are decelerated
by what the nurse infuses into her bruised vein.
These are the last-discovered things: umami, Pluto,
the masked facts of the way things are. We eat
meals alive with fish sauce. None of this is exotic.

Anne Ryland
After a Spell in Essex

In the summer I came back to the end of England,
my southern roots trailing behind.
Northumberland brooded; interrogated me:
how exactly would I contribute to its flintiness, its neither-nor-ness?
Unable to blether my way through

I roamed the claggy tracks
where lost peel towers guarded their secrets.
Marram grasses were no longer praying in the wind,
they were running away.
The sea didn't call me.

The rain warped my doors, and my inner walls ached as if a treasure
I never knew I'd harboured
had been removed.
My fault, for not shedding my birth county.
This land was in no rush – it swithered

till at shutter-closing time in November I sensed a faint crumbling,
and wrote a friendly letter to the stone women of Duddo
who'd been singing for four thousand winters;
professed myself Northumberland's hinny.
Though I still hadn't fathomed –

was a home on the border
a torment? A remedy?
I waited – and I nithered.

to nither – to shiver or huddle with cold

Stuart Charlesworth
So They Might Never Come this Way Again

Two children kneel in the room where one was born,
between packed boxes by a peeled-back carpet.
They are writing a message on the yellow,
exposed wooden floor.

Yellow for local wheat fields dusty with chaff –
they'd play there breaking stems – and the purple-brown
threadbare rug is for the estuary water –
boundary to their walks.

They're giant-children, crouched on the village's
corner like it's a man they've pinned prone. Long hair
streams in the sky; their faces angled towards
the flood defences.

Hands have clawed at land and water – laying bare
living earth. Humber waves race to ask the new
raw edges – *is a gift to be left here, or
has a grave been dug?*

Two children crouching, alone in a bedroom
made ready for a move. Gripping marker pens –
sharp-tipped syringes filled with dark-coloured drugs –
dripping on the boards,

        ready to send the house to a dreamless sleep.

Each child carefully writes their name and the date.
One adds *I was born here*, then side-by-side they
throw the carpet back.

Marion Tracy
Stones

He hears a sound, plip plop, it's small stones thrown
or wet insects on glass. The noise is getting bigger.
It sounds as if stones are being shovelled onto the house.
He asks his cousin if she has experienced anything like this.

He frowns when she says, *It must be possums.*
He smiles when his neighbour says, *Perhaps it's like*
when my wife left me. He laughs when his wife says,
Yes, I've been hearing it for a while, it's like memories of home.

He looks up through the leaves of the tree.
Stones are coming down through the branches.
Stones are bouncing off each branch in turn.
Stones are plums falling down like blue stars.

His neighbour looks and says, *Who can be responsible,*
is it the work of clever children? His cousin gasps and says,
Is it the work of aliens, these bright disks as they fall?
Is it, asks his wife, *all the words that need saying?*

In the room, the stones are all over the bed.
The stones are all over the rug but there's no holes
in the ceiling. He looks up and there's no footprints on the roof.
The stones are raining down and he asks his cousin,

Why do the stones not fall straight down but seem to turn in the air?
He asks his neighbour, *Why do the stones have no shadow?*
Why do the stones fall on my house and not on yours?
Why, laughs his wife, *it's all the stones that ever got stuck in my shoe.*

Amaan Hyder
At Hajj

He had been in his own group, walking in a line with his hands around the waist of the man in front. His group had been snaking through the crowds like that for a few days. One morning he had been at the back of the line and he had felt the crowds closing in. He had not seen it bottleneck so badly before. The message went down the line to hold on tight and he had got the sweat of the man in front on his beard.

Next to him a boy fell to his knees and he let go and helped the boy to his feet. The boy began to cry and he panicked and lifted him onto his shoulders and shouted as loud as he could in his language that the boy was lost. He yelled and the boy cried. He didn't know what to do. His group couldn't stop for him. A little while later the boy saw a familiar and scrambled into the hands of the pilgrims in between. He watched him go. It was over like that.

I've seen him asking around for his people, that man. The orphan. He had been in his own group, walking in a line with his hands around the waist of the man in front. He says in his language that he is lost. And watches while the message he sends out goes down the line like a boy scrambling on shoulders in a crowd. The scent bottlenecks at his beard and in his sleep he is lost and lifted and let go in the cried-out desert.

Bewketu Seyoum
Ah, my innocence

Ah, my innocence,
my gold-stained ignorance!
Instead of waiting for a bus,
I await the Messiah.
In a city full of monasteries,
in a desert full of mosques,
I hear the beating of wings:
is it an angel come to rescue the world?
or a vulture hungry for carcasses?

The door to freedom

Oh my dear spirit,
you make
your own laws,
run your own trials
own your own jail
and post yourself
your own guard –
still you are a prisoner
of your own power!
Instead of worrying
all night long:
"will he escape?
will he take his revenge?
what's he thinking?
what's he planning?"
why don't you free yourself now
by letting your captive go?

Zewdu Milikit
Year of the Spider

Animals symbolised years
since the olden days,
but animals are old hat now,
insects are the way to go!
It's the year of the Spider:
everyone's weaving a ladder
of cobwebs, and trying
to fly when they're falling.

Translated by Chris Beckett and Alemu Tebeje Ayele

Translator's note
I love the first reading of an Amharic poem, dictionary in hand, stepping into its train of thought, listening to the sound it makes. I like to discuss it with my friend Alemu over a beer. Then I try to turn my jottings into an English poem. Amharic is an inflected language, so its words are denser than English (e.g. one word, *ewedhallew*, for "I love you") and rhyme more easily. Plosive consonants bounce against the tracks of a regular six or twelve syllable line. Where possible, I use half-rhymes or assonance to imitate the original. How hard to convey both the sense and flare of an Amharic poem! Somehow, the shorter the train, the longer my journey of translation. – *Chris Beckett*

Patience Agbabi
The Doll's House

The source of the wealth that built Harewood is historical fact. There is nothing anyone can do to change the past, however appalling or regrettable that past might be. What we can do, however, what we must do, is engage with that legacy and in so doing stand a chance of having a positive effect on the future. – David Lascelles

Art is a lie that makes us realise truth. – Pablo Picasso

Welcome to my house, this stately home
where, below stairs, my father rules as chef:
confecting, out of sugar-flesh and -bone,
décor so fine, your tongue will treble clef
singing its name. Near-sighted and tone-deaf,
I smell-taste-touch; create each replica
in my mind's tongue. My name? Angelica.

This is my world, the world of haute cuisine:
high frosted ceilings, modelled on high art,
reflected in each carpet's rich design;
each bed, each armchair listed à la carte.
Come, fellow connoisseur of taste, let's start
below stairs, where you'll blacken your sweet tooth,
sucking a beauty whittled from harsh truth...

Mind your step! The stairway's worn and steep,
let your sixth senses merge in the half-light...
This muted corridor leads to the deep
recesses of the house. Here, to your right,
my father's realm of uncurbed appetite –
private! The whiff of strangers breaks his spell.
Now left, to the dead end. Stop! Can you smell

cinnamon, brown heat in the afternoon
of someone else's summer? This rust key
unlocks the passage to my tiny room,
stick-cabin, sound-proofed with a symphony
of cinnamon; shrine to olfactory
where I withdraw to paint in cordon bleu,
shape, recreate this house; in miniature.

All art is imitation: I'm a sculptor
of past-imperfect; hungry, I extract
molasses; de- and reconstruct high culture
from base material; blend art and fact
in every glazed and glistening artefact
housed in this doll's house. Stately home of sugar.
Of Demerara cubes secured with nougat.

Look at its hall bedecked with royal icing –
the ceiling's crossbones mirrored in the frieze,
the chimneypiece. The floor is sugar glazing
clear as a frozen lake. My centrepiece
statue of Eve, what a creative feast!
A crisp Pink Lady, sculpted with my teeth,
its toffee glaze filming the flesh beneath.

The music room's my favourite. I make music
by echoing design: the violet-rose
piped ceiling is the carpet's fine mosaic
of granulated violet and rose,
aimed to delight the eye, the tongue, the nose.
Even the tiny chairs are steeped in flavour
delicate as a demisemiquaver.

Taste, if you like, sweet as a mothertongue...
See how this bedroom echoes my refrain:
the chairs, the secretaire, commode, chaise longue,
four-poster bed, all carved from sugarcane;
even the curtains that adorn its frame,
chiselled from the bark, each lavish fold
drizzled with tiny threads of spun 'white gold'.

The library was hardest. How to forge
each candied volume wafer-thin, each word
burnt sugar. In the midnight hours, I'd gorge
on bubbling syrup, mouth its language; learned
the temperature at which burnt sugar burned,
turned sweet to bitter; inked a tiny passage
that overflowed into a secret passage,

the Middle Passage; made definitive
that muted walkway paved with sugar plate,
its sugar-paper walls hand-painted with
hieroglyphs invisible as sweat
but speaking volumes; leading to the sweet
peardrop of a stairwell down and down
to this same room of aromatic brown

in miniature. Here, connoisseur, I've set
the doll, rough hewn from sugarcane's sweet wood:
her choker, hardboiled sweets as black as jet;
her dress, molasses-rich; her features, hard.
This handcarved doll, with sugar in her blood —
Europe, the Caribbean, Africa;
baptised in sugar, named Angelica,

has built a tiny house in Demerara
sugar grains secured with sugarpaste,
each sculpted room a microscopic mirror
of its old self; and below stairs, she's placed
a blind doll with kaleidoscopic taste,
who boils, bakes, moulds, pipes, chisels, spins and blows
sugar, her art, the only tongue she knows.

'The Doll's House' was commissioned by Ilkley Literature Festival's 'Allegories of Power' project.

Miranda Yates
Chocolates for Colonel Gaddafi

Parents dance through the school doors bearing late marks,
Gaddafi is dead and they can hardly part from their yawning children.
There's the rest of their family's family's lives to lead from now on.

Ibrahim's Mummy wants her *Roses* for the kids acknowledged.
The newly qualified teacher is at a loss, he has had no training
in the culturally-sensitive handling of deposed dictators.
If there is a word for this gift, then that word must be 'inappropriate'.

Her hijab is skew-whiff and an emerald scarf slinks from her shoulder.
She steadies the top of her son's pencil, as he bears down
on his four-syllable surname, a rash of lines and wayward loops,
suggesting, for just a moment, that he has burst into fireworks of cursive.

Abdul-Malik from Year 1 sleeps against a wall during tidy up time,
two dinner ladies hug in the middle of Juniors' packed lunches.
The children leap at them like dogs who can smell a change in authority.

For the billionaire with the underground lair and golden gun –
fingers panning through gilt wrappers spread across the staffroom table.
For the Bedouin warrior, the mad dog of the desert –
a humble tin drum now empty, good for nothing but raffle tickets.

Mona Arshi
On Ellington Road

Old man Harvey, with his thick specs and polished shoes
shouting "trespassers" yet offering us a penny for collecting
his waspy pears.

Biji, looking old in widow-white, whose soft hands were always
stained with turmeric.

The achingly cool white brothers, who lived opposite with their
Mum and spent days fixing their motor-bikes.

Aunty Kamel, knocking on our door, with her black plait undone,
begging us to keep her for the night.

The Aroras, who had a real football pitch at the back of their garden
(Hounslow FC).

Cunny, Pummy, Bally and Kully (all boys).

The girl next door stealing her dad's razor and showing me how to
shave my legs with baby oil.

The white haired lady we called *Mum* at number 4, roaming the
fenceless gardens, until they brought her back in.

Dave, our young lodger, with his paisley cravat, smelling of Brut and
he had a car.

The boys in the gardens interrupting cricket games to scream at the
sky while Concorde flew by.

Meeting Renu, the new bride for my mum's cousin, and being scared
for her as I'd heard about what had happened in the launderette the
year before.

Manjit, aged nine, left in India as a baby arriving back to her parents, her
eyes black with kajal.

Several men from along the road setting up in our garden and building
the extension in just one day.

Being told off for climbing trees because "it was dangerous for girls"
and being told this by lots of women on the street.

My dad, insomniac shift-worker, blood-eyed, nursing his head in our
tiny kitchen.

ℬ

John Wedgwood Clarke
Identification

Laminaria digitata raises its thallus, holding fast with stipe
and branch and blade as a shout breaks in –
there, over there, mid-stream, in the tide race –
the names look up, dumbstruck, letting go.

Maria Jastrzębska
Fur

In the carved, oak wardrobe – so big
it stood in the corridor –
hung my mother's fur coat.

I crouched among spare shirt-collars,
old shoes and belts, careful
not to clink the bottles of barley wine.

My mother's scent was cloying, sweet
but I rubbed my cheek
on her fur, crossing the forest

of gaberdine, wool. I squeezed
between long dresses and coats
into a country of pines

where children wore crowns,
carried swords, rolled petrol-bombs
under the wheels of tanks.

On dark mornings I folded my bed,
kicked the ash of small fires
deep into the snow.

Hawks screamed above to warn me
when secret police were closing in.
No matter how cold it was

my huskies' breath was always warm.
On clear nights we crossed fjord
and steppe in a sledge.

I willed myself over distances –
past petrified deer and ice palaces
frozen lakes the size of oceans.

Safe in the whistling blizzard,
I left borders and villages behind,
rode towards the blue silence.

Magadan

On days when birds fell
from the sky like hail stones
frozen by the air itself

the sun was so small
it was as if it didn't know
how to warm the earth any more.

In all that whiteness they set out
past the fence, towards the empty plain
to pull beetroots from the hard ground.

On cold nights, as we burrow
under down, it seems
an indulgence to think of them

but I see their footprints in and out
of the perimeter. Follow them
as they're marched again

to lie next to each other
on wooden pallets. And what else
except this thought –

retrograde comet, its heat lost
in all that distance, the flare of its tail
still bright enough to be visible –

what else can I send back to them?

Ned Denny
Arles

You arrive in February, the darkness
of Paris forgotten in the sheer light
of fresh snowfall, the black outlines of trees
like Japanese script in whitened gardens.
It is near, the strange harvest of your life.
You make a study of an old woman,

receive a visit from some friendly men
who also paint, are struck by the darkness
of the local girls, find somewhere to live.
By April, the damp orchards are alight –
they sign to you across broken gardens –
with the upraised flames of transfigured trees.

In September, you sit amongst the trees
and watch as a blank-faced man and woman
shuffle their way through the public gardens,
the blue firs bristling with lupine darkness.
You are able to take a child's delight
in everything, seeing it all alive

(innocent of your gimcrack afterlife,
the Vincent erasers and mousemat trees
arrayed in the giftshop's shadowless light).
Your business is the salvation of man,
to wash from our eagle eyes the darkness
that stops us knowing ourselves in the Garden,

that keeps us pacing the madhouse garden.
You paint the blaring sun, broadcasting live
from the galaxy's wild hub of darkness.
You are drawn to the cypresses, those trees
whose ominous figures resemble men
in their spiralling journey up to light.

You write of the "blue depth" where the starlight
coils, of the jewels of that high garden;
you show no sign of the desperate man
who will voice the desire not to live,
illuminating this place of trees
where all's defined by a serpentine darkness.

*

When old men die, you said, they go on foot to light
from the darkness of these gardens.
We learn how to live by watching the trees.

Petra Kamula
Petra visits the Citadel of Aleppo

The Citadel of Aleppo is empty of the whole world except for you and I.

The Citadel of Aleppo is the colour of creamed honey.

The same colour sleep paints at the edge of your mouth when I am not awake to watch.

The stone the citadel is built on is an enormous hive above the flat back of the city.

In the honeycomb of the citadel you press your palms to huge wooden doors,
                    your hands light like the almond cakes we ate with mint tea
                    and black olives for breakfast.

You are wearing a yellow shirt. It hides your shape as the citadel hides its shape
                    from the people below, pulling up layers of colossal rock
                    to cover its shoulders.

From the top I can see the whole city, the lines of streets and the tracks of electric wires
                    intersecting and dividing
                    as if someone has taken a pen and crossed the whole city
                    out.

The cities of Aleppo and Damascus are our two hands roped together
                    on our way through the desert.

Your body within the neverending body of Aleppo, the oldest city.

In the hotel room you slide the yellow shirt over your head.
The tips of your fingers are anemones tasting the air beneath the thud of the fan
                    and the loose flood of aircon.

The straight ochre of your back.
The wings of your hips above me
                    a citadel rising to crown the city.

The nubbed staircase of your spine. I enter it
                    on my knees.

Your chin, tipped up like a cup of water
                    I will not get to taste.

Heidi Williamson
Descender

After Cavafy

Body, remember each
small, unwilled movement.
Each one is a fist or heel
of someone I will love.

Remember the way my skin
moves to my own amazement.
The way each reposition
ripples outwards into view.

This new person is already
working their way
towards me with a will
neither of us understands.

This small person will be
among us soon. Already
their lungs strengthen,
their skeleton lengthens.

As each tiny bone
readjusts constantly
to the given space – all
this, remember, body.

Laura Scott
Sewing

Sew until the light has left the sky.
Sew until your arm has found its grace
up and to the side, up and to the side.

Sew until the nape of your neck softens
as you turn to look at the leaves falling
on the other side of the glass.

Look at them falling into the night.
Someone has been here before you
with a thread thicker and blacker than yours,

squeezing it flat between finger and thumb.
Sew until you see the folds of her years
pulled into place by your stitch.

Christina Dunhill
Foraging

It's easy to lose us, raggedy children.
Your hands forget they held our hands,

your laps forget we sat on them.
You let our smell go sour.

Bad children, there isn't enough for us.
Where do we belong?

A bird sings in the imagined house.
Tap, tap, let us in.

If we were better, if we were golden,
it could be us there, hopping and singing.

Oh process

A makeshift workshop, near Lee station,
just a yard with walls you walked into from the street:
sickly smell of plastic melting, gravel crunch of granules,
roar of the moulding machines.

Four iron monsters, ugly and rusting,
four great machines for the four pretty plastics,
each machine with its own attendant, plunging a scoop
into her sack of granules, shovelling them into its throat.

Jostling, clattering, they swooshed to the smelt
to be slicked and smoothed into new moulded mass:
eye-shadow cases and tubes for stick deodorants –
pink, pale blue, white and lilac.

Oh process, oh transformation, petrol and its brainchild, plastic.
Oh gravity, oh centrifuge, oh heat and melting, smelt.
Oh shapeliness, form, and all casings: metal, plastic, flesh.

Valérie Rouzeau
from Vrouz

To meet your soulmate without paying afterwards

To meet your soulmate without paying afterwards
Till Sunday midnight minus one's impossible.
The midnight chimes ring out your pumpkin rolls
You home with one bare foot *exposé* to the cold
Of an endless winter's night. Time's running out
Its nasty rosary its sands its gallop through the dust
And now it's free so let's jump at the chance.
Don't miss this coach your love awaits
But code and password have both slipped your mind
You sieve-head singleton you dozy loner
Enter svp your pin your prick oh please
The spine that's in your sole the one you left
To wander bare one minute to in weather
Cold as this. It's midnight butterfly it's now or never.

Negative I don't know how to take a photo no

Negative I don't know how to take a photo no
Perhaps I ought to buy myself a phone
It's snowing and I watch the snowflakes fall
With an eye that's neither digital nor silvered
No desire to put things in a box I've no
Such moving magic no fix on the image no freeze-frame
I couldn't demonstrate my snow its mesmerising spell
Even if it is another cliché that I write
Like magical enchantment a few syllables poor flakes
If I could only catch them in a whirlwind
Of authentic *vrouz* delight before my heart should melt
Like a fox an owl an ermine lovely creatures
That transform themselves from summer into winter
Winter into summer beasts that can't be caught.

Swallow anything like nails or wood-screws ink

Swallow anything like nails or wood-screws ink
The keys of sardine-tins or shards of vinyl 33s
Pills of Nembutal or arsenic or phenobarbitone
Rolled-up super-stretchy braces real forged notes
In a Tartar izba hang yourself enough goodbye
From a knotted tie a spiral flex of phone
A skipping-rope to skip off in the void
A string a shoe-lace belt a ribbon of madame's
Or throw yourself from lofty bridges ledges Eiffel tower
Stick yourself with sword or chicken-skewer
Drown yourself in alcohol the leaden Seine the Thames
Get top marks as a marksman at the fairground stall
Open the gas-tap take a bath with blades
Everything can serve our ends trees rivers what the hell.

Translated from the French by Susan Wicks

Translator's note
When *Quand Je Me Deux* was published, the actor Jacques Bonnaffé apparently greeted it delightedly with the words, "Voici du vrouz!" – as if this contraction of the poet's name were itself the name of a language. This coined word is the one Valérie Rouzeau boldly chose to use as the title of her latest book, which recently won the prestigious Apollinaire Prize. It felt a great privilege to translate these sonnets. Not only because Rouzeau's work is so alive and original, but also because her whole relationship with language is dynamic and so forces me to reinvent my own. Trying to do her work justice in English is often a conundrum. Not least, the macaronics of "To meet your soulmate...", where the "please please" is actually in English in the French original, as of course is the source of part of the wordplay on "pin / pine / épine". Hence my daring to keep "s'il vous plaît" in its shortened form and import the punning French "exposé", which I hoped might produce an "authentic vrouz" smile. It's not all delight, though, as the packed literary references of 'Swallow anything...' will testify.

Selima Hill
The Iridescent Conversation Piece

(for David Batterham)

When I see the frantic little legs,
I whisper to the frantic little fly

she'ld make the most desirable – if legless –
iridescent conversation piece,

and as I speak she seems to move away,
ankle-deep in syrup though she is,

as if she knows I'm so *beneath contempt*
for going on and on about desiring things.

John McCullough
The Sugar Hammer

weigh its riddle in your palm – burnished steel
so slender it gathers just enough force to rupture
a loaf for a gentleman's tea, knock-knocking
as if asking permission to fall deeper and harder
and hand-made – cast fondly and pounded itself
so it knows how it feels,

                     a knowledge you'll taste
in the iron of the flat, honest blows as it opens
you up with those tremors, a high-voltage
rush to the head, an intimate conspiracy,
your own hand on the turned fruitwood handle,
uncertain who's hammer, who's sugar
as it all strikes and quivers, all swings
through the air, leaving sweetness in its wake

Mike Saunders
Suitcasing

Another one arrived on Sunday,
a fax, from Kent Park Holiday &
Conference Centre. He sends one
every time, always with the coda:
I'll make a fan of you yet!

He almost has. My favourite pen,
ink thinner than a standard biro,
is courtesy of Amari Hotels &
Resorts. I have a postcard
stuck to the wall behind my desk

sent to me personally from
The Fiesta Resort Group – a woman
holding a bowl of something,
smiling off to the upper left
suggesting I "get away from it all".

But this isn't what he means by a fan.
He means *You will come to love
anonymity* and *You will often
write tender letters to room cleaners.*
He means *last time, in Europe,*

*I waited until dark and crept through
the connecting door to the master suite
in soft complimentary slippers
and took the Italian newspaper
from the nightstand next to the bed.*

Ángel González
Zero City

An uprising.
Then a war.
In those two years – a fifth
of my whole life –
I experienced different sensations.
Later I imagined
what fighting means as a grown man.
But as a child,
the war, for me, was merely:
school lessons suspended,
little Isabel in panties in the basement,
car cemeteries, empty
apartments, an indefinable hunger,
blood found
on the earth or a street's paving stones,
a terror that lasted
as long as the weak rumble of glass
after the explosion,
and the barely comprehensible
pain of adults,
their tears, their fright,
their choked anger,
which, through a few cracks,
entered my soul
to then vanish, quickly,
before one of the many
daily wonders: finding
a still-hot bullet,
a nearby building
struck by flames,
the leftovers of looting

– papers and framed portraits
in the middle of the road...
It all went by,
it is all blurry now, all
but what I hardly perceived
at the time
and which, years later,
reappeared in me, now forever:
this hazy fear,
this sudden wrath,
this unpredictable
and real need to cry.

It's What Happens, Sometimes, in October

When nothing occurs,
and summer is gone,
and leaves start to fall off the trees,
and the cold rusts the edges of rivers,
and slows down the flow of waters;

when the sky seems a violent sea,
and birds swap landscapes,
and words sound more and more distant,
like whispers strewn by the wind;

then,
as you know,
it's what happens:

those leaves, birds, clouds,
strewn words and rivers,
fill us with sudden restlessness
and despair.

Don't seek the cause in your hearts.
It is merely what I said:
what happens.

Translated by Gonzalo Melchor

Translator's note
Ángel González (1925-2008) belonged to the so-called Spanish Generation of 1950 who grew up during the Civil War and in Franco's ensuing dictatorship. As a result, González, in his own words: "learnt from an early age to protest in whispers, to curse inwardly and to speak ambiguously, very little and always of other things – that is to say, to use irony, metaphor, metonymy and reticence", all of which are trademarks of his dark, humorous and incisive poems. The translations aim to carry across González's unique voice, reflecting his sound patterning, expressive lineation and personal blend of poetic and vernacular diction.

Helen Oswald
Last Will

The first year, we pulled up
beetroot, purple and wisp-haired
as a newborn's head, peeped
at broad bean embryos incubating
in cotton wool, pricked out lettuce,
their green hats so frilly we guessed
dames tottered underground. We eased
shy dynasties of King Edwards
naked into the spotlight and, sensing
their shame, led them to safety
deep inside our own darkness.

We did not know all this was thanks
to fallow years; that fat harvests
would one day end. So,
if I cannot keep conjuring
this magic, my love, mutating
afresh into other lives – bury me
in thin soil beside the cankerous
old apple tree and leave
this exhausted tilth to rest. Trust
I can wait until the earth dreams up
new ways for me to be.

Jane Griffiths
Found Object

Her first view was buddleia and Bramley.
The sky was silk-skein and a long way off.

Its grass-and-wind smell blew with the wind
which came and went. It was true north.

Her second was river, broad and industrious,
strong-arming its barges and container freight.

It was here she dropped a small brass coin:
knew it lost, but *lost somewhere in the world.*

In her mind's eye it was centred, like a pupil.

Her third view was building site, a dream
of brick repeating brick. It was treelessness

and puddle. Its smell of mud persisted.
She could make head nor tail of it,

though there was skating, some months,
and each spring, marbles: hoards of them,

circled on their still-stopped lava flows,
lost and won in pockets of the earth.

She took a pocketful for compass the day
she left to hunt a sky recognisably itself –

which would be north, she thought, or across
the river. Sometimes when the wind changed

she could see it, almost, as through the eye of –

Carol Rumens
The Death of King Taharqa

For Aisling Lavery

As long as the Pharaoh wants the war
the war wants the Pharaoh.
When the Pharaoh wants the war no longer,
he sinks back on his haunches, already a sphinx –
prayed to, lied to, a vessel
of bandaged promises –
and the drum, the drum he hates
(why must it beat so hard, this weightless heart?)
slips under his feet, devolves
to remembered footfall.

*

These are my rhythms – footfall and waterfall:
The steady capable beat, and none at all...

The river my sister sings the shape of herself,
leaps where the lion leaps, leaps past the lion
on his short rope, appetite:
stretches and broadens, hungering northwards and seawards,
grass-river, snake-river, sky-river
sun-written, stilled under stifling papyrus;
rousing and racing the lion-man-river-man's racing,
water-fall, foot-flash, rainbow-flake, neck-and-neck,
tumbling past settlements, lolling in rock-pools, black
and white in the granite stairwells, slow and smoke-yellow
through Memphis and into *hundred-gated Thebes.*

The Kushite cub, foam-furred, boundless, god-sent,
found something he'd never touched
before – a girl's hinged mirror
                              drawn from his ribs
when he saw the sand-drowned temples
                        bright with pity.

*

Now the lion's outrun, done in.
He sags on his flank, panting,
where the unfledged papyrus sighs
for sunlight, twisting its toes
in the foul canopic silt;
where the night-boat waits for the god some call Amun,
and he calls Kawa.

When the
         Pharaoh
                Wants the
                        War

when the pharaoh
                wants the war   no longer

*

souls panic and clatter
like netted marsh-birds, blind
to everything but their sky.
Don't let them see me, know me.
This was my lion army,
its wounds, cut by Assyrian iron (but I willed them),
dark-red, viridian, jagged as butterflies.

Croak with the broken ibis, Pharaoh. Howl with the soldiers' wives.

*

Waves move in from nowhere, heaving the marsh.
Even the dead roll over. Kawa, Kawa!
The night-boat's solid sunlight, bright as the day-boat,
and the god's a diamond cloud. The cloud disembarks
and blazes towards me over the ash-dark jetty.
I can't look into his face, but I hear his language, flashing:
Aren't they the Pharaoh's army?
What's the story, Pharaoh?
Clothe them in memory, Pharaoh.
Taharqa, gather your men.

*

I dig out my roar, the old drill-sergeant's blather.
The bones crawl, the sinews twist together.

Here's my battalion, yearning
into the sun, reviving,
growing in moments tall – pure spectacle
for the god, as he
messes about like a boy,
spins time, sets everything racing.
They stand, wheat-perfect, quivering,
stunned by the white-hot cloud.
I goad them. *Who's your god?*
Who taught you to run, those silk-cool desert-nights,
to run for the sake of the war
until he wanted   (wiser than Xerxes)   wanted
to call off the war   no longer
wanted the war   (but dared not)?

*

Those nights of the moon-marathons, we were no-one –
joggers un-armed, un-ranked, bit of a joke.
At first we yelled and buffeted each other,
but soon with a fiercer beat and concentration
we ran, ran on, ran on and on, our lungs
tight lyres, we rubbed the burning from our eyes
which filled and burned at once, till smears of palm-tree
formed like ghosts out of the pale dawn sky.
And the victor crashed the finishing rope, and flung
himself across, and we
flung ourselves anywhere, laughing
or weeping, lightly-wounded pride the same
for slave or king, runner-up or also-ran.

We praised each other, thanked the gods, we plunged
our mouths in bowls of pomegranate wine,
and it seemed the light wrote on the broken stelae
of ripples where we skinny-dipped, and each
to his own unscripted face said *Kawa! Amun!*

*

By the river that rises in the Otherworld
where everyone's god is his heart, mixing him freshly
from blood and darkness,
                         drumming him lightly
                                        drumming him

to rise and run with his pride
                         I am the Pharaoh
      of whom the scribes wrote this:
                         He flung the molten ball Jerusalem
                         into the future. Memphis he returned
                         to the priests.
         And this:
                         Taharqa ran with his men.

                    *

They run, Taharqa runs, for the joy of hard breathing,
for the thunder of soles on sand, for the butterfly victory:

for the god in the dream – his moment in the hand.

Note: "Kawa" abbreviates 'Amani of Kawa,' the Kushite form of the Egyptian sun-god,
Amun (pronounced with the second syllable stressed).

Katrina Porteous
It Will Pass

O the temporariness
Of grief
By which we weather it.

O temporariness,
Spring of all grief.

Kit Fan
Zurbarán's Window

I

There are midsummer days when the twenty-four
suns drink up all the wells in Fuente de Cantos.
Even the maps are eaten up by the shadows.

So, come along. Turn right, then left, at the cul-de-sac
of a cobbled street. In the house of buttons, ribbons
and needles, the son of a haberdasher is drawing.

His hand says sky, and it turns charcoal blue.
His hand says clouds, and they turn charcoal rain.
His hand says mother, but she keeps sewing by the window.

II

Twenty-four years later, he looks into another window
where he puts a sewing basket by her ruby dress
and a single teardrop on her brooding face

as she sees her son braid a crown of thorns,
the matter-of-factness of his thumb teasing a thorn
out; a drop of blood on the index finger yet to be licked off

says God is in the detail. Slip in for a second,
mind the salt-glazed bowl by his bare feet. The window
in the house at Nazareth says it's raining in Fuente de Cantos.

Rebecca Farmer
The Angel of The Flies

By the look in your eyes I see my disguise is a shock.
You'd expected something white and feathered
maybe a dove, but the way I see it, fractured though it may be,
a fly is perfect because I've come to feed on death, your biggest fear.
If not yours then someone you love.
Sorry I'm laughing, but your face looks like a total eclipse.

Julian Stannard
Burlington Arcade

I'm being carried down
the Burlington Arcade
by Beadles in top hats,
jewellers on both sides
holding out their hands
and wrapped in cashmere.
When people speak of
near-death experiences
they're always going through
tunnels, they're happy,
they're never going through
the Burlington Arcade.

Eric says, It's good
to see you wearing clothes
and I have to admit he's
wearing the most beautiful
trousers and I say, Eric
you're not supposed to be
in this poem. Get back
into your shop! I can see
a light at the end of the tunnel.
The Head Beadle's saying
'Burlington Gardens!'

Should I tip him?
Am I dead?
What happens next?

Dorothy Sargent Rosenberg Annual Poetry Prizes

PRIZE WINNERS FOR OUR 2012 COMPETITION, ANNOUNCED FEBRUARY 5, 2013

$7,500 to Leslie Elizabeth Adams, Michelle Y. Burke,
Nina Riggs, Brittney Scott, Ali Shapiro and Sam Taylor
$5,000 to Josh Booton, Jenny George, Tess Jolly, Kerry Kwock and Rebecca Macijeski
$2,500 to Ameerah Arjanee, Ruth Awad, Michael Boccardo, Jodie Childers, Brieghan Gardner,
Rochelle Hurt, Courtney Kampa, Tracey Knapp, Hannah Oberman-Breindel and Matthew Thorburn
$1,000 to Anders Carlson-Wee, Weston Cutter, Adam Fell, Dana Koster and Brittany Perham.

There were also thirteen Honourable Mentions at $250 each.

THANK YOU TO EVERYONE WHO ENTERED AND CONGRATULATIONS TO OUR WINNERS

WE NOW HAPPILY ANNOUNCE OUR

2013 Competition

Prizes ranging from $1,000 up to as much as $25,000 will be awarded for the finest lyric
poems celebrating the human spirit. The contest is open to all writers, published or unpublished,
who will be under the age of 40 on November 6, 2013. Entries must be postmarked on or before the
first Saturday in October (October 5, 2013). Only previously unpublished poems are eligible for prizes.
Names of prize winners will be published on our website on February 5, 2014, together with
a selection of the winning poems. Please visit our website www.DorothyPrizes.org for further
information and to read poems by previous winners. Please note that our deadline for entries
is earlier than in previous years and that we have a new mailing address.

CHECKLIST OF CONTEST GUIDELINES
- Entries must be postmarked on or before October 5, 2013.
- Past winners may re-enter until their prizes total in excess of $25,000.
- All entrants must be under the age of 40 on November 6, 2013.
- Submissions must be original, previously unpublished, and in English:
  no translations, please.
- Each entrant may submit one to three separate poems.
- Only one of the poems may be more than thirty lines in length.
- Each poem must be printed on a separate sheet.
- Submit two copies of each entry with your name, address, phone number
  and email address clearly marked on each page of one copy only.
- Include an index card with your name, address, phone number and
  email address and the titles of each of your submitted poems.
- Include a $10 entry fee payable to the Dorothy Sargent Rosenberg Memorial
  Fund. (This fee is not required for entrants resident outside the USA)
- Poems will not be returned. Include a stamped addressed envelope
  if you wish us to acknowledge receipt of your entry.

**MAIL ENTRIES TO: DOROTHY SARGENT ROSENBERG POETRY PRIZES
PO BOX 148, STEWARTS POINT, CALIFORNIA 95480, USA**

Centrefold

❦

...a poem is a haunting: a disembodied
voice shackled in type.

– Jen Hadfield

The Anonymous Invitation
Eight New Poems by Unnamed Poets

NOTES FROM THE EDITORS

Having had what seemed like a simple idea, the logistics of putting together the Anonymous section were interesting. Firstly, we wondered whom we should ask, and then worried about whether they'd be hostile to the notion – after all, publication in *Poetry Review*, even for established poets, is generally a cause for celebration and fanfare. In the event, we were delighted that most of the poets we approached were able to accept, and were, in fact, intrigued in a variety of ways by the concept. We're very grateful to them for their willingness to take on this unusual editorial request, and for their generosity and talent in providing us with such a fine set of poems.

The eight poets who took part are all established and there's an even split between women and men. We encouraged them to write something new for the commission to test if the cloak of anonymity affected their creative process in any way, or to take this as an opportunity to send us a poem where they had tried something they considered rather different from their previous work. In addition, we asked them to provide any thoughts they had on the experience of writing/publishing anonymously and you'll see there's a fascinating range of reactions, from those who felt it had little impact to those who found it liberating or unnerving. Finally we gave them the choice of remaining permanently anonymous or having their identities revealed in the Summer edition of *Poetry Review*, allowing them an interval to decide whether they'd like to 'claim' their poem at a later date. Watch this space!

As a concluding note, we should say that, at the time of writing, the poets' identities are known only to us as the editors and to staff at the Poetry Society, whom it was necessary to inform for purely practical reasons – the poets remain anonymous to each other. Beyond the fun of trying to match poets to poems, we hope that readers will be intrigued by the experience of encountering these poems against the white field of their own making.

ℬ

Anon. Poet I
The Storm

Was I always like this, a watcher first and a doer second?
Twenty children ran from the house to greet the storm.

But not me. I stayed on the porch and studied them.
They cartwheeled as lightning rolled dice overhead.

Something crawled under my skin for me to join them;
An impulse that I had to fight to keep in check.

I looked at the nearest grown-up to make doubly sure
It was all right and saw no reaction, just watchfulness,

A peer up at the blackness thickening and a glance at us,
And not much more than a pulling close of an open shirt.

And so I dived off the front porch and into field grass
With the others and pitched defiance (gobbled up by

The hungry wind throwing its weight around)
At the strapping dark, whistling trees, pushing them

This way and that for fun, with twigs and leaves torn
And flung in our faces and water lashed at us.

As lightning squared up directly overhead, white sheets
Cast wide and deep with us for fish to gather up,

Aunts and uncles called us in, and the stragglers by name.
We filled all the windows for the rest of the show.

We were loud, jittery, spastic, giddy, and at one
With the storm whose current ran in us and made us

Beg to go back out in the open, to throw up our arms
For the wind and the lightning to claim us all

As their offspring and drag us up into their embrace,
Beyond the reach of adults calling, calling our names.

Anon. Poet I writes: A commission to be anonymous is like the invitation from hell: you don't ever want to go there though you won't mind finding out a bit about the place. In this instance the result is a poem that originates in the spark of a memory but owes much of its art to the imagination (Eliot's visions and revisions, I suppose). The artist-figure who watches the making of the memory ends up being the one who fashions it into art. There is something of sociology's participant-observer to all this. The poet lives the experience and, simultaneously, imagines it as art. That posture of hesitant participant may be the hardwired condition of the artist in life as much as that life inhabiting the artist. The two-way street (many ways, many streets) makes it hard to do anything more than simply obey the signs of the poem when it arrives, and asks to be fleshed out and be made more of than the bare bones of recollection. The nervous system of the poem translates as the emotional reality for the poet. The success or otherwise of the poem can be gauged or measured by the extent to which the reader picks up on the poet's declared architecture of feelings. Or not. I wish I could have just read the invitation and not attended the party. But it turns out that these invites appear in disguise since they are really offers made to the imagination that are too good and therefore cannot be refused.

℘

Anon. Poet II
Sciurus Carolinensis

Sun rivers on glass, threatens to mount, blaze
into my eyeline so that, heat-struck, I headlong

down to hump squirrelled in the shade below, leaves
moving as I move, as grass moves with the snake.

I am the grey. Born helpless, blind and deaf.
My mother lays me across her forepaws, fetches me

out of a cave, weans me once my teeth appear.
Sciurus names only my *skia*, shadow, *oura*, tail.

I displace the red. Acorn-bred, carrier of the pox,
I infect it with lesions, ulcers, scabs, weeping crusts,

it shivers, shivers, *skia*, *oura*, and then it's dead.
I mean no harm. I'm no image seared on your brain

only seen side on, tail up, ears tufted like conifer spurs;
no nutkin on a branch, jug on a wall, graphic loop,

no ampersand between presentiment and trace.
Skia, *oura*, I flicker on the walls of the cave.

Anon. Poet II writes: I was very happy to be invited to submit a poem for the anonymous section of Poetry Review. It feels quite joyful to be nameless, without the baggage of biography and history, much as it does wandering around in airports once you've checked in and are suddenly unburdened. Every poet wishes to get out of the way of his poem and this is a welcome step further. Freed of the writer's or reader's expectations, prior knowledge, cultural frameworks, the poem can stand, ageless, genderless, before us and newly introduce itself. Although a poet's work necessarily leans on its biographical and critical context, it is always revealing to see how a single poem fares when it is orphaned. I look forward to reading the other anonymous poems in this bold and intriguing editorial project.

ℬ

NOTE: *The following pair of poems comes from a poetic dialogue between two poets.*

Anon. Poet III
43

buried in play, before winter
arrives in quills & sets out its case

rolled up in last resort, stripped
down to heart rot of a peeled twig

sounding of ash, coppiced to
the finality of endings   nilled

sourcings of voice, here she
sends back echoes   where

tunnels & fingertips take you
through the darkness to meet

the sudden purge of light, that
point where it began   to tread

a path, she finds principle
& die-back, diamond

canker, marked out

Anon. Poet IV
44

sourcings of voice: window, door, streetlight,
branch scraped and rattled, pod, rain,
wings of wind   so voice, so the sudden

purge
and then nothing, space and nothing, voice
and nothing gaps   here we live in this

in this and that and the winter blanched
unbranched like the sky a white space and grey
and swart and indigo and then and then

so she, child, voice like undersong, heard
through window, door, streetlight, sourcings

of wind and sudden and purge

and this is where this is where voice

breaks and holds its sustaining path,
principle, play, quill, tunnel, ash

Anon. Poets III & IV write: The project involves us writing alternating poems, each a response to the last. Having agreed a starting point of 28 lines, we decided to move through ever fewer lines until we got to one line, and then reverse the process. The broad subject was fixed by the very first ekphrastic poem that had in mind a specific painting deliberately withheld from the other poet. That painting was loaded with certain associations, material texture, colour. The next poem picked elements of the first to riff on and develop, and so it continued, touching and prompting beyond habitual practice. Anonymous is the most productive of poets and we are pleased to be adding to such a magnificent oeuvre. Going without names is also what people on the internet do a good deal of the time – the billion-headed monster is composed of a billion mouths and twice that number of ears. These poems pop out of two of such mouths more naked than they would normally be in the company of their names. Let them live on their naked wits and hearts.

Anon. Poet V
PG Deaths

When hero shoots pulley they are buried under a pile of chain;
one hand protrudes, twitches, twitches, goes limp.
They drown in syrup / sump oil / treacle, gurgling
because viscosity is funny; we cannot say why.
They slap the ground in frustration and fall out of shot,
eternally incapacitated. A child murders them.
They are pointing out the Pleiades to an ermine-wrapped
starlet when the crane they booby-trapped last season
swings and knocks them both off the promenade
to be conked by a love boat. They are made into taffy
or jerky or both. Their weakness of spirit addicts them
to a volatile and difficult to source recreational drug,
a tainted dose of which dissolves their throat, salt on ice.
A bowling ball rolls down an ironing board and strikes a match
and etc. etc. etc. etc. etc. etc. etc. etc. severe clinical depression.
The hero refers to their demise in parenthesis.
They are crushed by falling novelties / brightly coloured
exotic fruits / vast ivory button. They are thrown in a bin.
A single rogue castor from the falling piano winched
above the hero's tenement ricochets off a fire hydrant
and into their temple. Flattened by the elephant they abused.
They fall into an industrial mincer to be blended into a fine paste,
the company logo incongruously jocular.
The camera pans left and accidentally slices them in half
against the side of a mountain. Racism gives them a heart attack.
Representative from a minority group to whom
they have previously expressed prejudice
lands killing blow with ironically appropriate object.
Following head injury they develop artistic ambitions,
and death, a useful formalist – and silly, and wise –
comes to nobody but the unjust who asked for it.

Anon. Poet V writes: The first image comes from that Arnold Schwarzenegger / Danny DeVito comedy *Twins*. I was talking to a friend about the scene where the villain dies and that, while suffocating under a pile of chain must be a pretty horrible death, it's necessarily played for laughs. That in PG films death has this clownish presence, so (bad) characters still have to die for the story to have a conclusion, but the writer has to do this without upsetting the young audience or raising any difficult questions. This probably sounds like a truism, but I think you write all that you're capable of writing. I've certainly never written a poem I wasn't capable of writing, and that's not for lack of trying. I've never spoken to a writer who feels as though they have a brand to uphold, so that writing anonymously might liberate them from that. But I have spoken to writers, including myself, who are prone to lapsing into self-parody, but I think I can say with conviction that writing anonymously hasn't liberated me from that at all. Which in the absence of a self is maybe death by self-parody.

Anon. Poet VI
Notes on the Enemy

after W.H. Auden, from 'Journal of an Airman'

Three enemy coats – black to the calf on Sundays – reversible anorak –
> dripping cagoule.

Three enemy faces – white – harmless – man & woman interchangeable.

Three enemy voices – whisper – rumour – sermon.

Three enemy weapons – orphans – Jesus – ABBA.

Three enemy strategies – Saltire on a 100ft pole – Boden –
> flowers on the doorstep.

Three enemy codes – 3 for 2 tea lights inscribed with a prayer –
> embrace – ☺ over the 'i'.

Three front lines – frozen beach – herbaceous border – window.

Three battle conditions – incandescent – grey – apocalyptic.

Three signs of enemy victory – swans – leaves falling in spring –
> swollen congregation.

Three enemy celebrations – shit through the letterbox – dancing
> on the ceiling – solemn cheering.

Three lines of defence – Jubilee bunting – leylandii – blinds (handmade
> in one night from nettles).

Three casualties – air – life – nation.

Anon. Poet VI writes: : Between 1929 and 1931 W.H. Auden taught at a small school in the west of Scotland. During this time T.S. Eliot accepted his first book for publication and he wrote 'The Orators', arguably his first major piece of writing. 'The Orators' contains many references to the area he was living in as an outsider. My poem responds to a section from 'The Orators', taking Auden's theme and mood of surreal paranoia and bringing it into the present day. This poem thrived under the strictures of the Anon. invitation because anonymity gave me freedom to write about what I wanted to, unfettered by concerns about how readers might relate the poet and the poem, and it also creates an interesting uncertainty around the poem.

Anon. Poet VII
Fall

That was our most inspired decision:
escape from perpetual love –
the taste of our insipid sin
still on our tongues –
into the giddiness of separation.

Once in the world of random things,
away from those complacent borders,
dazzled by all this changing,
we've found our own language,
the drunken freedom to be wrong.

Perfection made us restless,
created human as we were.
It was His choice – to make us
lower than the angels,
with imaginings beyond our grasp

and incapable of constant happiness.
Here, it is the permanent erasure
of each day; it is death, loss,
that render luminous each detail
of this urgent, fragile universe.

It never rained in heaven.
Here, our very breath returns to us
as dew. We shield our skin
prepared to feel the blizzard in our hair.
We fly! We leap! We run!

Anon. Poet VII writes: The invitation to provide an anonymous poem for the spring issue of Poetry Review was, at first, exciting. The possibility of writing as someone of the opposite gender, for instance, or in the style of some other poet, or in a form I have never used opened up the prospect of discovering a new voice, a different direction. But I soon came to feel that I had been given almost too much licence, and none of those tempting, playful possibilities produced a convincing poem. In the end, I relinquished the attempt and wrote a poem in my own, possibly characteristic, way – though not in my own voice. Curiously, preoccupation with the issue of how much freedom one can handle seems to have given rise to the poem. Adam and Eve are euphoric at having escaped the predictable constraints of heaven. But perhaps, if the poem were to have a sequel, we would find their joy tempered with disorientation and regret. Who knows!

ℬ

Anon. Poet VIII
With Two Young Cats, New Year's Day, 4am

After the party, the three of us are hunkered-down
in a moonlit scullery, a household asleep above.

Twin nocturnes; they stare back bright-green the light
their blackness captures. Their world is full of unknowns

to which the answer is always *lick fur cleaner.*
I love these young killers: their brazen innocence,

their comic ignorance of their beauty. Somewhere
a year is turning, but this ink and silver hour

is theirs, their alien time-zone. They move and freeze
as one; resting now, heads lowered, eyes just-green

in threshold reverie, listening to things
I'll never hear, listening to the moonlight.

Anon. Poet VIII declined to comment on their anonymous poem.

Said, Unsaid & Mr Nobody
Micro-essays on the power of the Unsaid and the Anonymous in poetry

JEN HADFIELD

Yesterday, upon the stair
I met a man who wasn't there
He wasn't there again today
I wish, I wish he'd go away

('Antigonish', William Hughes Mearns)

1.

The unsaid is not absent. It is palpable. It can give rise to a pernicious medical condition. You're stranded in your body, as if on a motorway roundabout, ringed by accelerating minor aches and pains. I know: there are things I need to say that I'm not saying. They are palpable. When I present at the surgery with my apparently hypochondriac array of mysterious chronic symptoms, the ultrasounds, urine-dips and blood-tests come back clear. My doctor palpates the unsaid through my stomach-wall. Do you know what happens to the thing you must say, but are not saying? It silts up – as trauma does – in exactly the muscles you would've used to articulate it.

*

How much of the human body is recruited in a simple, uninhibited utterance? (How many simple, uninhibited utterances have you produced in your life to date?) Ask a friend where they think their voice comes from and they are likely to say – even as their brain orders their diaphragm to dilate – something like *my voice comes from the voicebox/my larynx/the vocal chords*. But that's like saying the ignition is what makes your car run. A simple, uninhibited utterance depends upon an incredibly intricate series of impulses, co-ordinations, contractions, recoils, oscillations and resonances. The uninhibited voice employs, in the end, most of the body.[1]

*

A smile can be a snarl of the unsaid. It stiffens under the face and scalp like

---

1. See 'How the Voice Works' in *freeing the natural voice*, Kristin Linklater, Nick Hern Books, London, 2006.

drying mud. At times of social or emotional tension, the unsaid is a small clay ball, like an oolith or baking bead, wadded over the hinge of my jaw. It aches and stiffens my smile.

*

Our bodies are proficient in reading the unsaid, even when we don't notice that that's what we're doing. It's like reading strata in sedimentary rock. And some of this unsaid is ancient. Some of it is inherited. Some of it we salted away in the first six months of life. And because all forms of language are contagious, we readily contract somebody else's unsaid. "Your mother's cross because I drank too much: she gave me the silent words."

*

On the third day of the course, 'Freeing the Poet's Voice', Kristin Linklater turned us to face the window that overlooks Loch Long. She directed our gaze through the crowns of the trees, over the tense, dull ripples, to the military vessel herded fore and aft by tugs, to muddy, shallowing wavelets, to the lean beach littered with sanitary waste and plastic lighters. We were to imagine that there on the beach stood our good friend, Gai-Gai. "Shout, 'Hi, Gai-Gai!'" instructed Kristin. I gave a strangulated, breaking half-shout, inadequate and disproportionately desolate.

*

To call but expect no answer, to have the deep-rooted belief, founded upon nothing, that nobody is coming. For some of us, for a variety of biographical and cultural reasons, a simple shout is a near impossibility. This seems to be very normal in my culture. There are many possible causes for an etiolated voice. The most primal is identified by Bruce Chatwin:

> Visitors to a baby ward in hospital are often surprised by the silence. Yet, if the mother really has abandoned the child, its only chance of survival is to shut its mouth.
>
> (*The Songlines*, Bruce Chatwin)

*

The doubt that a parent will hear the baby's cry can become a doubt, in later life, that anyone is listening. Calling becomes unsafe. Speech is effortful, embarrassing and exhausting. How many poetics originate from this primal fear or its mutations in later life? The one who most wants to call may be the one who goes to the greatest lengths not to, perhaps because spoken language has become too arduous to use, or because he/she has the most to lose:

> Did she think of me [...] Did I pause, switch off the desklamp and
> stand, gazing out at the dusk, think I might call her. Not calling.
> Calling. Too late now.
>
> (*Men in the Off-Hours*, Anne Carson)

*

Don Paterson proposes "Poetry [...] is not a calling but a diagnosis."[2] I can't shake the conviction that poetry more often than not represents the urgent discharge of language from those who find it hardest to speak. The germ of 'Freeing the Poet's Voice' was the observation that poets are often the worst performers of their own work. Is this because the people who have badly needed to speak are the ones who have relied upon writing as a safe substitute for the risky acts of articulation?

*

> Who listens
> like lichen listens
> assiduous millions
> of black and golden ears?
>
> You hear and remember –
> I'm speaking
> to the lichen.
>
> The little ears prunk
> scorch and blacken.
>
> The little golden mouths
> gape.

*

Emily Dickinson reputedly conversed with visitors, if at all, from the other side of a closed door.

*

---

2. 'A post-Creative Scotland', *The Herald*, 14 September 2012 and forthcoming in *Unstated: Writers on Scottish Independence*, WordPower, 2012.

> Then it was over: that which you fear, being
> a soul and unable
> to speak, ending abruptly [...]
>
> I tell you I could speak again: whatever
> returns from oblivion returns
> to find a voice.
>
> ('The Wild Iris', Louise Glück)

2.

I react to a poem as I do to a person. A poem isn't a poem unless it is also a piece of spoken language, albeit scored on the page – a collaborative act between writer and reader. It possesses many of the characteristics and, I think, the courtesies, of a true conversation. The person who talks over me, who crams every beat with talk and will not let me take breath (while the unsaid presses painfully on my jaw) is like the poem that wants to tell you everything. The true poem is an act of individual negotiation with the individual reader: white space, breath-pause and mystery all invite digestion and reply.

*

> There is something you should know.
> And the right way to know it
> is by a cherrying of the mind.

The reader creates meaning in collaboration with the poet, in the following way: where room is left for the unsaid, where language is to some degree gnomic (as in Anne Carson's 'First Chaldaic Oracle', above) or meaning only partially revealed, the poem is viable: i.e. it can still be negotiated between writer and reader. This is the opportunity that Carson – in the wake of her mother's death – values in Virginia Woolf's "cross-outs":

> Cross-outs are something you rarely see in published texts. They
> are like death: by a simple stroke – all is lost, yet still there. [...]
> Cross-outs sustain me now.
>
> (*Men in the Off-Hours*, Anne Carson)

*

Does the published poem sometimes forget that it is a spoken and not a written language? Emily Dickinson mistrusted publication, too, suggesting that in publication, a poem loses a kind of virginity, is transformed into a commodity:

> We – would rather
> From Our Garret go
> White – Unto the White Creator –
> Than invest – Our Snow –[3]

*

I often meet students who are excited to have been introduced to the Rules of Poetry. They have received the good news that their writing could be economically transformed into poetry if they excise a variety of species of extraneous matter: all the adjectives and adverbs (and articles, if they want to write haiku), all the clichés, and self-conscious poeticisms. The Rules help a new writer take a squall of messy, live language and pat it rapidly into the shape of a poem. But I so often have a funny feeling about the end product. Something has been occluded, fossilised, cauterised. The flow of what has been stemmed here? The connection with what has been constricted?

*

Emily Dickinson's dashes:

> Dickinson uses dashes musically, but also to create a sense of the indefinite, a different kind of pause, an interruption of thought [...] to join two thoughts together or pushing them apart.[4]

I don't really think I have much to say about those dashes that is new. Of course the most interesting are those which don't obviously signal a parenthesis, or have a straightforward musical motivation. I'm just thinking   what if   those dashes that her poems so often 'end' with and the ones that make a line a rusty splutter from an outside tap what   if they don't instruct as to how she means the line to be delivered, but instead, how it was delivered to her?

3.

> I'm Nobody! Who are you?
> Are you – Nobody – Too?
> Then there's a pair of us?
> Don't tell! they'd advertise, you know!

Those leading dashes with which so many of Dickinson's poems end. As if all

---

3. 709, *The Complete Poems*, Emily Dickinson, ed. Johnson, Faber, 1975.
4. *Poets.org Guide to Emily Dickinson's Collected Poems*, The Academy of American Poets.

the poems were really one, and the dash a temporary respite in the current of dictation.

*

Once or twice I've been invited to read from my poetry for an hour – usually in a university, or in Germany, where poetry audiences seem to have more stamina. An hour-long reading is a barrel-scraping exercise. The poems I still read are the few that still feel relevant to who I am now. A very few. They were the ones that always read best, and that sometimes make me cry in public, as you sometimes do when you speak rhythmic words in unison with a roomful of people.

*

'Nigh-No-Place', 'Iamb', 'Paternoster', 'In the Same Way'. That new one, 'Lichen' – that gave me hope. These are the poems that I never intended to write. They're my white snow if I have any. I'm not sure I did write them. The other poems: they look ok on the page, but taste like fibs. I intended, directed and edited them in all the right ways, and I think that's the problem.

*

That sensation of being dictated to is the reason I still try and write poetry. Who is that? Mr Nobody? One way or another, a poem is a haunting: a disembodied voice shackled in type.

*

One of Linklater's useful maxims: "get out of the way of the poem".

*

After four days and nights uninhibiting and reinhabiting our loosening bodies, we didn't recognise ourselves or each other. We *did* I think recognise our poems as we'd first felt compelled to write them. On the final night we sat up late and drank and sang, and Edward Mackay made extraordinary tea-lights out of satsumas, with the pith for a wick.

Non-smokers met on the balcony and rolled fags for each other. An owl called. As the night wore on we missed our friend Gai-Gai and proposed to call him out. On the count of three, our prehensile voice whanged across the loch and over the submarine base like a rubber lasso, and reverberated off the mountain's bare bosses and corries.

Jen Hadfield lives, writes, gathers and makes in Shetland. She blogs intermittently at rogueseeds.blogspot.com.

Work in Progress

LINDA FRANCE

When it was pointed out to me that 2013 would be the twentieth anniversary of the publication of *Sixty Women Poets*, it was like getting one of those out-of-the-blue emails from someone you knew at school: a sensation of time cracking open, a great chasm between then and now, me clinging on to the edge. I felt caught in the chaos of work in progress; the task of fairly representing the state of contemporary women's poetry still unfinished.

I dedicated *Sixty Women Poets*, published by Bloodaxe in 1993, to the women in my Women's Group, who have been meeting since 1986. It seemed fitting to attempt a twenty-year review in the same spirit of solidarity and continuity. I asked various women poets I'm in touch with to chip in, keen to hear their views on a book it's hard for me to be entirely objective about and on the wider subject of their experience as women poets in 2013. To begin, here is a representative selection of their responses to the impact of the anthology on their lives:

> Ground-breaking... Part of the poetic landscape I grew up with... Permission and recognition... A permanent vindication... Encouragement to explore the work of other women poets... A sense of community... Inspiration and hope... One of the key books on my shelf... A constant resource... Redressing the balance... A comprehensive overview... An important way for women to value each other's work... Raised profile of women poets, made us feel part of a wider world... An excellent introduction to contemporary women's poetry... An intriguing selection... Well-thumbed.

It was always my intention for the anthology to be a celebration of the diversity of women's voices, a tracing of the genealogy. That process had already started with Carol Rumens's *Making for the Open: The Chatto Book of Post-Feminist Poetry 1964-1984* (1985) and Fleur Adcock's *Faber Book of 20th Century Women's Verse* (1987) – both important books for women in the eighties, hungry for words that illuminated our own. From across the Atlantic we were nourished by the commentaries of Tillie Olsen and Adrienne Rich, but still trying to break our own "dream of a common language" (Rich). Writing since I was a teenager at a girls' grammar school and working in Women's Education, I was at ease with the idea and practice of women-only forums for awareness-raising and mutual support. I had an equal commitment to poetry and feminism, and that ideological background was reflected in how I approached the editing. It is interesting to note how often American women, beyond the scope of *Sixty Women Poets*, were cited as major influences upon the women poets I consulted: Elizabeth Bishop, Denise Levertov, Sharon Olds, Sylvia Plath and Adrienne Rich were recurring names.

Revisiting *Sixty Women Poets* has been like opening "a basket loud with wings" (Annemarie Austin). Even though I carry many of the individual poems around in my head, I found returning to them gathered all together deeply affecting. There's a strong sense of women in conversation with each other, "a voice answering a voice" (Virginia Woolf). There is music in it, harmony, rather than simply noise. And lots of energy – curious, provocative and irrepressible – that reminds me of a remark of Selima Hill's: "the best thing about writing poetry is the same as the best thing about being alive".

Re-reading my introduction I notice myself striving to be clear and conscientious in presenting the patterns I detected in how women were writing then, in the two decades since Stevie Smith's death in 1971. It was important to me, too, that the poems were accessible, allowing doors so many women had felt shut in their faces to be unlocked. In 1993 a women-only anthology was a necessary act of correction, of positive discrimination.

My decision to order it alphabetically rather than by age, I now see has happily resulted in the selection being bookended by Fleur Adcock and Anne Stevenson, two important and influential poets, still writing at the height of their powers. There are certain poets I regret omitting, particularly Ruth Fainlight, Sarah Maguire and Kathleen Raine; there is only one, however, I regret including. The difficulty was always with numbers: the *Fifty* originally suggested by Neil Astley quickly rising to *Sixty*, which could possibly have run to *Seventy*. The sheer quantity of women worth reading, the majority of whom had published two full-length collections, had a powerful effect on women as readers and writers. With so many women poets in one place there was no possibility of any spurious sense of unity. It was even perversely satisfying to be able to add the note regretting that Sheenagh Pugh was "not willing to be represented in this book because she refuses to have her poetry published in women's anthologies". Women poets, as well as being different from men poets, were different from each other – a fact taken for granted now.

Sixty Women Poets was published at a time before the internet, and also before the boom in MAs and many poets finding employment within academia. It was a selection chosen by a young mother in her early thirties. This bestows an air of innocence upon the book and also dates it. However, as a woman in her mid-fifties, on the brink of grandmotherhood, I'm struck by how much harking back there is in the media currently to issues we were discussing in the seventies and eighties – assertiveness, abortion, body image, equal representation, violence against women etc. Even though we were shocked by the General Synod's voting against women bishops, maybe we weren't surprised. Everything is different and everything is the same.

It's hard to imagine a 'mainstream' women-only anthology being published in 2013. Drawing serious attention to gender inequality seems to have lost cultural momentum. Women have become very good at acting as if they were equal. It might be indistinguishable from the real thing, until the dry ice clears and a continuing divide is revealed. According to the women poets I consulted, there are still reasons to be disappointed:

> Men's poetry tends to be more widely reviewed... More women attend readings by male poets than men attend women's readings... There is still a sense that poetry written by men sets a standard, determines a quality level... Poetry is a genre that is notoriously bad at promoting itself and particularly bad at promoting women.

To my mind, poetry is a genre that also offers the possibility of hope. Always good in a crisis, it is a place of authenticity that can at least imagine positive change, a world where silences can be broken. Women poets' voices are being heard more clearly – in print, on the radio, winning prizes, judging prizes, editing magazines and anthologies, writing articles, speaking for themselves (and for the three nations – Carol Ann Duffy, Liz Lochhead and Gillian Clarke). Women are writing and discussing issues of interest to both sexes, no longer just 'women's work'. It is particularly refreshing to hear women poets with the authority, on the radio and in print, to discuss the work of male poets, a rarer phenomenon in 1993. Women poets committed to their own practice are transforming themselves and each other, what poetry is capable of and the culture it feeds.

I have considered the status of women's poetry post-*Sixty Women Poets* in *Binary Myths 2*, edited by Andy Brown (Stride, 1999), and for the Newcastle Centre for Literary Arts online magazine *Friction* (2010). The strongest continuing thread seems to be an abiding sense of diversity, reflected in and reflecting women's willingness to engage with each other's work, to offer exchange and support. I am lucky enough to be a member of a women's poetry group, based at Newcastle University, which has been meeting in different configurations since *Writing Women* magazine was an important touchstone in the republic of women's writing three decades or so ago. Currently consisting of Linda Anderson, Christy Ducker, Cynthia Fuller, Pippa Little, Lisa Matthews, Ellen Phethean, Anne Ryland, Anna Woodford and myself, the group meets once a month to 'workshop' poems in progress. This is a valuable and sustaining forum it would be hard now for me to live without, with a particular dynamic only possible in a women-only environment.

The North has long been a law unto itself, and well known for its tradition of strong women. It is a fertile place to work as a poet – of either gender. One of the major issues for women writing, however, both among published poets and beginners, is still confidence, not helped by the wider media's distorted representations and expectations of women, young and old. Lack of confidence is perhaps the main obstacle to women not being more visible or authoritative. From her experience as Editor at *Poetry London*, Colette Bryce has said "submitting work to a magazine, risking rejection, *risking success*, is active," compared to the more passive mode of a tutor-led creative writing workshop. *Mslexia* magazine, based in the North East, was founded to address the reluctance of women writers to seek publication, offering advice, encouragement and opportunities. Women's spaces – workshops, classes and magazines – are still useful for inspiring confidence, nurturing new work that is so vulnerable to external pressures, mundane and insidious. That is not to say this is not an issue for male poets too. "As life's outsiders," according to Lorna Thorpe, doesn't "exclusion and invisibility... come with the territory" for poets, whatever their gender? Jane Hirshfield suggests: "We are most comfortable being hidden but we yearn to be seen."

Jackie Wills wonders if the idea of a non-competitive community of poets, regardless of gender, is too idealistic. Nevertheless, this hasn't stopped her, with Ros Barber, taking the practical, affirmative step of establishing *A-gender*, an online database of women poets in the UK:

> We did this to show how many women poets there are. We had no funding or backing for it and got it going with some voluntary support, then hoped that women would contribute their own profiles based on our criteria – a woman needs to be writing in the UK and have published at least one collection.

This needs proper funding to be developed further, updated and edited.

I concluded my introduction to *Sixty Women Poets* with a quotation from Marguerite Duras: "The truth is what I think sometimes, on some days about some things." I stand by that sentiment – especially on matters related to poetry. In the past few years, however, things have discernibly shifted. We have worked towards equality in both poetry and the society out of which it comes. To a large degree in poetry at least, what we see now, on the surface, is probably what equality based on diversity looks like. Lorna Thorpe wonders if "there might never have been a better time to be a woman poet". For Anna Woodford "'poet' is still the all-important noun". But whatever the balance, we are still struggling within structures that have been created from a patriarchal viewpoint, hierarchical and competitive, from which none but a privileged few benefit, male or female.

What is different now from the situation in 1993 is that we are seeing signs of the possibility of radical change – not just in poetry but in every area of contemporary life. The tumultuous pressures arising from the struggle between the conservative and the co-operative, the evolutionary and the ecological, don't make comfortable viewing, but the grandmother in me would like to think that eventually some good will come of it, out of sheer necessity if nothing else. At a time of global environmental and economic crisis, there are, in Marianne Moore's words, "things that are important beyond all this fiddle". But still poetry has something to offer – its "place for the genuine" (Moore). Its natural myth- and image-making, clear perspective and carefully articulated rhythms might not be *all* we need at a time when society is lost, in the dark place between one cycle and the next, but re-imagining difference is a good place to start. As Ali Smith puts it, open-endedly, in *Artful* (Hamish Hamilton, 2012):

> Here's to the place where reality and the imagination meet, whose exchange, whose dialogue, allows us not just to imagine an unreal different world but also a real different world – to match reality with possibili

With thanks to Colette Bryce, Cynthia Fuller, Ellen Phethean, Anne Ryland, Lorna Thorpe, Jackie Wills, Anna Woodford, quoted here, and all the other poets who responded to my queries.

Linda France's blog is poeticabotanica.wordpress.com. Her latest collection is *You are Her* (Arc, 2010).

ℬ

Black Silent Waters

TIM LIARDET

Ever since I first read him, Ted Hughes has been for me the remote dark-eyed and intercessional figure. By that I mean the presence in the rain-shadow of which I had to learn how to grow my trade, often resting my head on the pillow in a state of knowing I would never please him sufficiently – the presence which first blocked the way, then cleared it. I came across Hughes in 1988 and the effect was softly devastating. I'd turned to poetry as autodidact and had read little more than Yeats, Eliot and De La Mare's old man "...pottering in his thoughts". Then I heard this:

> [...] how loud and above what
> Furious spaces of fire do these distracting devils
> Orgy and hosanna, under what wilderness
> Of black silent waters weep.
>
> ('Thrushes')

What? It was the clamouring gutturals and packed form that made this seem like a foreign language which so vibrated in me I already spoke it fluently. The West Yorkshire vowels could be heard, it seemed, mulching with soft Massachusetts inflections. There were the adjectives which stooped like boughs of fruit. There was the deeply male, Wagnerian diction and the unashamed afflatus. The iambs were loaded. This seemed, in short, the *ex cathedra* voice of poetic masculinity, understood in a flash. A probing of darkness was its species of ancient courage. Language, it stated, was not a passive medium but had to wrestle with its subject-matter and be allowed to *show*. What the proposition lacked in humility, it made up for in power. Though it probably sounds trite to say it, I knew I'd never be the same again. All these years later, I am still recovering. Such writing had the organ pipes authority of Milton coupled with the sort of energy and newness that Billy Connolly claimed overwhelmed him when he first heard Elvis sing *Heartbreak Hotel*. The writing had Milton's density, but was shaggier; it had Elvis's hip-movements but danced even more suggestively.

In this way Hughes became my ground bass. In the years since, other influences were added like melodies which were imaginatively developed above the Hughesian bass line. From Peter Porter, I learned the lesson of masculine suavity, and was given permission, often expressly, to be 'difficult'.

From Redgrove I learned how to harness a sensual apprehension of the world; from Lawrence Durrell how to place a filter through which masculinised emotion might be strained; from William Golding a sense of momentum. Many women poets (including Emily Dickinson, Amy Clampitt and Sharon Olds) were stirred in. All of them understood male diction's preoccupation with the iamb; all of them recognised the crushing patriarchy of language while simultaneously subverting and transforming it. Courage, tempered by humility, was the principal force.

Any voice has to find the subject which most makes it talk authoritatively. When I taught for a year in a Young Offenders' Prison my poetics collided in broad daylight with the subject it had been waiting for: a male writer tackling an exclusively male universe. The result was *The Blood Choir*, published in 2006. During this year I was forced to confront myself as cloistered boy set adrift in an institution which robbed me of my language and insisted I invent a new one with sufficient tact to tackle the prison's ascetic reality. Under the buckling atmospheric pressure of incarceration it developed its own way of speaking. The imprisoned men and I were unquestionably two species of male; to offer them the expansiveness of poetry was beside the point:

> I felt like a man sent to fix, say,
> a ten-by-three mile rupture in the side of the Zambezi dam
> with a tube of calk, dental floss, a hammer and nails
> and an endless chain of paper bags that filled up and burst;
> the thrown-into-the-gap, the heaped, the washed away,
> as quickly dissolving sandbags of woeful words.

There was no scope for board-marker and agenda, so I sat among them, listening. As if a valve had opened, I produced more poems than ever before in a twelve month period. I had to find a language which expressed the chill of the prison and which could remain true to the young men I was writing about; to show the way in which some of them seemed touched by a sort of eerie grace. In the end, individuals were fabricated in poems, often composites built out of at least five men, but nonetheless three-dimensionally real. I endeavoured to explore the nature of the cultural distance that existed between us: what became clear was that I was not writing about prison so much as masculinity under pressure.

Though I didn't know it at the time, I had found the intercessional subject. After *The Blood Choir* came *The Storm House* – a book-length elegy for a dead brother – which further waded the depths of twenty-first century masculinity. Bigger demands were made of the language in this book. It had to incorporate patterns of male cruelty passed down from generation to generation through the lens of evolutionary psychology; it had to explore the perils of male sensitivity; it had to tackle the North face of the father-son/mother-son relationship. It had to tackle the language of grief and attempt a lopsided, brother-to-brother discourse.

In a polysexual age of transgender, third gender and genderqueer shifts in identity, gender seems to evaporate the moment it is touched. Masculinity fragments into *masculinities*; each of these breeds its own mysterious forms. This remains for me the subject through which I must find a way. My next full collection due 2014 – *Portrait in the Gaudi Mirror* – will explore such proliferation. It will contain a sequence of letters to Peter Porter and several dreamsongs to Hughes and to the ghostly figure known as "Uncle Ruth". Each of these represents a point in the construction of the masculine psyche. In one of the 'Letters to Peter Porter', down in the London Underground, the carriage is full of noise:

> I couldn't quite make out what you said.
> For every word the racket could smother
> I cannot be sure but I would say you said
> *...In life we have many sorts of father.*

Tim Liardet's new pamphlet, *Madame Sasoo Goes Bathing*, is due early this year; a new collection is due in 2014 and a *New and Selected Poems* in 2015, both from Carcanet.

Tim Liardet
The Rain-Charm

...the shaman returns with all kinds of things
      – Ted Hughes, Letter to Moelwyn Merchant, June 1990

Tall as a church, he was tall as a church
stooping over my crib. He stooped,
he leant, where his upper half could lurch
the rest of him into view and shift his weight
from one hand to the other. I saw the pulse
bulge in his wrist, bulge and race;
when he leant, when he stooped, his gaze
implied the prospect of grace;
then, as his torch yawed, of something else.

Upside down, it revealed how
he dwelt in his features. The straight,
possibly angry line of the mouth below
the philtrum's furrow, dark to one side,
the spider veins in his cheek.
When he looked over, his face filled with blood
and became less face than flesh-mask;
he'd suffused his clothes, it seemed, which shed
a peaty odour elevated to a reek.

There was ear-hair, there were sideburns
in need of pruning, leggy and overgrown.
There were eyebrows crosshatched like thorns
reaching but not meeting;
there was the stray, forehead jib
of hair which fell away, until he brushed it back.
The torch was dropped, picked up, then flooded
my face: "...I am Crag Jack's
grandson come to lift you from the crib."

His old jacket seethed with microbes,
there was a patch on one elbow but not the other,
a briar-scratch on his earlobe;
his fingernails were chipped, as hard as horn,
there was moss in his socks;
his trousers were soaked to the waist, clung-to by seeds
of the meadow-grass he'd waded,
brushed by the laden reeds;
and, in his hair-roots, ticks.

It was Pastor Hughes come calling, I thought.
When the torch-beam skidded
and squirted up so he was caught
first at that angle, then this,
I shivered, sensed his pupils dilate:
...for a moment I thought it was my father.
That squelch, squelch as he walked
suggested he had crossed in waders
at the widest point of the river, now in spate.

When he sighed and spoke his voice
provoked, soothed, provoked and soothed:
there was intensity, there was excess
and both were carried forward in his sigh.
The shaggier, riper, overripe
vowels rolled around, the tongue
struck the back of the teeth;
the 't's fell like gutter-drips among
whatever else was shuffled to his lip

when he read to me—while I slept—
what seemed like a lesson and my sleeping brain
caught what signal it could intercept.
It was like a growly recording, played
to me in sleep, in delta sleep,
a voice now fulsome, now terse
played to fingers which rapidly copied it.
"Dream", he said, "the black verse
which shakes but cannot break your sleep.

See, I have deep pockets. Here's what I found in there
for you. This will be our secret.
My lush and pendulous voice will wear
through you a runnel, the drip,
drip of it on the sternum will cut a groove
deeper and deeper. Even when
you've no idea what you're saying
(and may simply whisper a soft amen)
your mouth will start to move

like a mouth at first miming then trying
to speak. At first you'll copy
every cadence and every dying
fall, I know. As if to bite the hand that fed
and cajoled and guided you,
at length you'll spurn the source. The lip-sync
will lose the lips. The time
will come when you'll think
it was you who said what I said."

Pop-up: the support system of the poetry workshop

JACKIE WILLS

Silence, a table with ten people round it all writing, or reading, until one talks... these components, so familiar to many poets, can change lives, and their impact may burn slowly for years. They are, of course, the components of a workshop, one of the most established support systems for experienced poets and new writers alike.

During an intense decade of running workshops, I have witnessed how they influence individuals and society, the way we work together and alone. In schools and during residencies with Unilever, I realised the power of the space a workshop creates – changing dynamics in an established group, helping a new group cohere, altering how people perceive one another at work, suggesting a new self-image.

I became aware of the transformations – social, personal and creative – that happen as a result of a workshop, which is so often the butt of jokes, dismissed by cynics, even an embarrassment.

More than twenty years ago, Eavan Boland made a passionate case for the power of poetry workshops to influence the discourse within Irish poetry. She argued they were an agent of change for people denied permission to call themselves poets – those who were not male, white and middle class. She commented: "I have met, who hasn't in this world – arrogant and complacent poets. I have yet to meet an arrogant and complacent workshop."

American poet Lorenzo Thomas believed the Umbra writing workshop he belonged to in nineteen sixties New York with Ishmael Reed, Calvin Herton and many others was indeed part of one of the continent's most momentous changes. He argued that this collective of young black poets was one of the catalysts for the Black Arts Movement that precipitated the formation of black publishing companies, magazines and theatre groups throughout the US.

Thomas wrote: "The young black writers in those years approached their work with a sense of outrage and with a missionary zeal borrowed from the Southern Civil Rights struggle and heightened by an urgency bred by their urban surroundings."

Struggle, urgency, zeal – these are states I have encountered often in poetry workshops. The struggle of young asylum seekers at a hostel in

Chichester who leapt on my copy of Benjamin Zephaniah's *Too Black, Too Strong*; the zeal of a young teacher making links between William Blake, Alan Ginsberg, Bob Dylan and John Milton and encouraging his pupils to write their own songs of experience; the struggle of young people in a secure unit to express their lives behind fences and locks; the urgency of the words all of them delivered.

In 2002, poet Sarah Maguire set up a poetry translation workshop at the School of Oriental and African Studies in London. Two years later it became the Poetry Translation Centre for contemporary poetry from Africa, Asia and Latin America. The Centre has been instrumental in widening access to poets whose work was inaccessible to many of us and our experience is radically altered.

I've seen other changes too – strong emotional reactions, pride, a sense of achievement, something communicated that had been buried, an insight that surprised even the writer. I've seen a group form out of a random collection of individuals. It is why writing workshops are so often integrated into community programmes to provide an activity that gives those involved new choices in how they perceive themselves and how they respond to others, germinating social change.

The workshop is a focus, then, for a community of interest, of passion and belief. Its structure, so flexible, seems to be one that can be packed up and opened out in almost any situation – pop-up before the term was invented. A good workshop encourages experience to be articulated beautifully, surprisingly and it has two hinges: insight and competence. By nurturing these skills, the workshop becomes a place where individuals' insight grows through sharing work, reading closely and developing an understanding of what works linguistically, by concentrating on the line, the word, punctuation, the arrangement on a page. Individual competence and the awareness of craft evolve within the workshop community of people with different approaches, themes and aesthetics. The work-in-progress group that so many poets belong to exists for this creative development.

Some of these groups are legendary – Philip Hobsbaum established the Belfast and London Groups and his workshop model, close reading of members' work, has been followed since the 1950s. Nobel laureate Seamus Heaney once reflected, "What happened Monday night after Monday night in the Hobsbaums' flat in Fitzwilliam Street somehow ratified the activity of writing for all of us who shared it."

In 2011, Michael Longley also remembered the power of that group: "It's a convection current, which you get caught in and it lifts everybody up. If somebody writes a terrific poem it's an incredible incentive to his or her colleagues to do the same."

This work-in-progress model is often a closed or invited group but the other model centred on creative change is the workshop delivered by a facilitator. It has many manifestations – from Michael Laskey's famous mass workshop at the Aldeburgh Poetry Festival, to Peter and Ann Sansom's events at The Poetry Business. Ann-Marie Fyfe's themed workshops at the Troubadour in London encourage a combination of close reading and writing, and in Brighton, Maria Jastrzębska and John McCullough of Queer Writing South are providing a supportive space for LGBT writers. Hundreds of experienced workshop leaders work in the community, education and business, and books by Cliff Yates, Pie Corbett, Matthew Sweeney, Peter Sansom, Sandy Brownjohn, Kenneth Koch, full of writing exercises, reflect the workshop experience. Notably, for most of these poets, reading and writing are inseparable.

The launch of Ruth Padel's BBC Radio 4 workshops, *Guardian* and Faber masterclasses surely indicate the workshop's popularity. The rise of creative writing degrees and masters programmes extend it into academia.

So what is the workshop's broader appeal? Is it the shared experience of discovering new poets, delicious silence around a table, the concentration of listening, a realisation that words, ideas, metaphors are infinite? Or is there something indefinable? A good workshop dismisses as irrelevant the debate about whether writing can be taught – with an experience like that, who cares?

I've run workshops under scrutiny in business, education and for arts professionals, where I've felt pressure to quantify results and assess their impact. I've taken feedback forms along, been sent charts showing participants' reactions, done Action Learning and been put under the microscope for the *Harvard Business Review*. While the immediate impact of a workshop is often startling, I believe that longer term it establishes an approach to making work that explains the existence of many artist groups – an approach that is centred on process and insight, the paramount importance of language.

The personal support that workshops offer is also powerful. Often people sign up at critical stages of life. I've witnessed this on countless occasions. The workshop is a springboard – the play, talk, listening, criticism and concentration can influence an individual's approach to creativity for life.

When I was invited to go to the Avignon festival as part of a team of gallery educators to experience how French animateurs work in Les Centres d'Entraînement aux Méthodes d'Éducation Active (CEMÉA) it confirmed my belief in the process. CEMÉA promotes self-development through activity. The workshops I participated in there were not explained but I felt their impact and as I watched performances later, I experienced another level of understanding. I made the links, drew conclusions myself.

A writing workshop shows a nine-year-old, a medical student, an underachieving teenager, a marketing executive, how writing happens, how to listen, observe, mimic, create and that is what they take away, not someone explaining in bullet points how a writer works. My own formative experiences were in a series of writing workshops in 1986 with Matthew Sweeney, on Arvon courses, and in a one-off workshop Liz Lochhead ran at the Southbank Centre, London.

Not every workshop is overtly therapeutic, but many factors at play within a therapeutic group (as documented by Irving Yalom) feel undoubtedly present in a writing workshop: a writer feels less alone, more confident, is able to take risks, learns from others, may be able to express emotion more freely.

Pioneers of workshops as therapy in the UK include poets Graham Hartill, Fiona Sampson, Victoria Field, Christina Dunhill and many others who have developed a therapeutic model, as in drama and music. But outside this specialist area, I've witnessed workshops building groups and self-confidence, empowering people to write about something they'd buried, discovering a talent for writing they were unaware of, rediscovering the pleasure of reading. Philip Gross perceptively describes the workshop as "a complex culture that demands alertness".

Some writers can't bear the idea of a workshop and at times in my life I didn't have the strength for the close scrutiny of a group. But I'm a member of two now, and they allow me to re-evaluate my work and to experiment. A good workshop is based on trust, it's small, critically tuned, it focuses on care, craft, what works, what doesn't. For some, a workshop is part of an apprenticeship, for others an entertainment or diversion. But most of all, it's based on kindness – not in a saccharine, unable-to-name the fault way – but it balances our insecurities against the demands of our craft, the need to edit, revise and improve the poems that can arrive so unexpectedly.

References
Eavan Boland, 'In Defence of Workshops', *The Poetry Ireland Review*, No 31 (Winter-Spring 1991) pp 40-48
Lorenzo Thomas, 'The Shadow World: New York's Umbra Workshop and Origins of the Black Arts Movement', *Callaloo*, No. 4 (Oct., 1978), pp. 53-72
Philip Gross, 'Small Worlds: What Works in Workshops If and When They Do?' in Diane Donnelly (ed) *Does The Writing Workshop Still Work?* Multilingual Matters, Bristol (2010)
'The Belfast Group: A Symposium,' *The Honest Ulsterman*, No. 53 (Nov/Dec., 1976)
Susan Mansfield, 'Michael Longley – Shadows of mortality', *Edinburgh Festival Previews* 16 August 2011, Scotsman.com

Jackie Wills is writing a guide to running workshops. She is also working on a fifth collection of poetry, *Woman's Head as Jug*.

Quality Time

John Greening remembers Dennis O'Driscoll,
who died on Christmas Eve 2012

During a literary lunch to celebrate a new BBC poetry anthology in 1995, a bearded fellow leant across to me and muttered, in mild Irish accents, "You realise that we are sitting opposite the author of the most popular poem of the twentieth century..." He was talking about Jenny Joseph, the speaker was Dennis O'Driscoll, and this was the first time we had ever met. It was typical of the man to draw attention to someone else's achievement; typical of him to point out something so quietly remarkable. That, indeed, was what he could do as a poet, gently gesturing to something obvious which we'd not slowed down enough to notice before. Bread and butter, perhaps ("A harvest loaf with / ornamental bark to carve through and reveal its inner grain; / leaving a trail of crumbs, like sawdust, on the breadboard.") or simply that "Charles Ives symphony improvised on the spot" which is the background music of our everyday lives.

I quickly learnt that Dennis knew everyone in the poetry world, had any touchstone you might ask for in his pockets, and was a conversationalist capable of connecting everything with everything. Since I lived in Cambridgeshire and he in Dublin, there would never be enough such conversation and our own connectedness (he didn't really do email) would depend largely on handwritten letters and virtual encounters at the literary stock exchange of magazine and small press. Yet – as that Merovingian script of his might suggest, the characters at once huge and fastidious – Dennis never overlooked important details even as he saw the bigger picture, which is why some twenty years after our first meeting he would draw the best out of Ireland's Nobel Laureate. Those interviews with Seamus Heaney in *Stepping Stones* (and it is, after all, the intelligence and selflessness of the questioning that set up such fascinating answers) would become Dennis O'Driscoll's most widely read work, although his wonderful anthologies of quotations brought him a good deal of attention, too. In fact, one could compile a pithy *Bloodaxe Book of Dennis O'Driscoll*: "Poetry is hand-crafted language in a mechanised world"... "poetry for most people is like the Christmas tree that is kept in the attic and is taken down at its appropriate season"... "The angel of 1990s poetry is the fairy of 1890s poetry"... "poetry is something like [a part-time fireman's siren] – if the siren goes off, you have to interrupt whatever you are doing and respond to the call". His brilliant reviews and extended essays on poetry (together with some of those epigrammatic *Obiter Poetica*) are collected in *Troubled Thoughts, Majestic Dreams* from Gallery Press. His utterly unegotistical gaze illuminates a huge variety of poets, shifting with ease between his beloved Elizabethans and any number of contemporary Eastern Europeans, alluding en route to some surprising figures (a Ronald Duncan here, a Valentin Iremonger there), alert to the politics as well as the personalities and, of course, the poetics – although he makes a point of going easy on close analysis, giving critical theory a wide berth. Dennis did not have a conventional education, having been plunged into full-time work as a civil servant when he was sixteen, but he read vastly and his critical insights came from true passion, not from any academic sausage machine. He knew, in other words, what writing is for, and that readers are busy people.

Although he was never what might be called a headline act, it is pleasing to think that Dennis O'Driscoll's own performance as a poet did not go unrecognised. Indeed, the Lannan Award is probably the most welcome tribute (in every sense) short of a Nobel Prize. When he received it in 1999 it enabled him to find, as he said in a subsequent interview

> the perfect balance between life and art, between my Customs desk with its reams of laws, tariffs, regulations and instructions and my poetry desk where the pages are blank, instructions are irrelevant and every new poem is a law unto itself.

That poems can be a law unto themselves is true enough, as the viral history of 'Warning' shows us, and Dennis did produce some poems that (like Jenny Joseph's ageing purple woman) began to take on a life of their own. 'The Bottom Line' in particular had him talked about in circles beyond those reserved for poets. He touched a nerve among the chattering classes and had a way of writing about the workplace that even that other celebrated nine-to-fiver Dana Gioia could not equal. Whereas Yeats believed that "sex and the dead" were the only fit subjects for poetry, Dennis O'Driscoll might have said "work and death". In the poem 'Someone', sex is naturally there, but it takes its place in the anaphoric routine: it has happened, been granted passing attention, while for the protagonist the only immediate concern is work. For poet and reader, however, death is the theme. We are the ones with the proleptic gift, relishing the marble and that terminal salute:

someone is dressing up for death today, a change of skirt or tie
eating a final feast of buttered sliced pan, tea
scarcely having noticed the erection that was his last
shaving his face to marble for the icy laying out
spraying with deodorant her coarse armpit grass
someone today is leaving home on business
saluting, terminally, the neighbours who will join the cortege...

'Someone', which opens Dennis O'Driscoll's *New and Selected* was much quoted when the news of his death emerged (he died on Christmas Eve; New Year's Day would have been his fifty-ninth birthday), although there are dozens of his poems which might have had a similar effect. The preoccupation with mortality was already ironic enough for one whose first job was in the Death Duties office. Yet it was understandable in a poet who lost his own parents very early and whose life choices were, as a result, strictly limited (he suddenly became responsible for his younger siblings). Now – as he himself would have been the first to point out – he has outdone the Yeats of Auden's elegy: the death of the poet has converged with the poems; he has become his own subject.

By the time he and I began to correspond, Dennis O'Driscoll was already a poet whose books I looked forward to. He would unfailingly send me a copy of his latest Anvil collection, inscribed with some allusion to our shared vintage (both born 1954) or some other warm-hearted remark ("to a fellow poetry omnivore"). And I would return the favour. Every writer needs someone who will read what they have written in the way they hoped. He was the ideal reader – and an obsessive one, as his partner Julie O'Callaghan shows, when (in her poem 'Bookworm') she opens a cabinet under the kitchen sink and is "surprised to find / you leaning against a water pipe / reading *Myth and Ted Hughes*". He said he had no time for television ("too literal") and even found music got in the way of the poetry. Who could not but admire such dedication?

It was in 1997, after Richard Murphy's seventieth birthday event in the National Gallery, Dublin, that I feel we really became friends. A colleague and I had brought some sixth formers over for a literary tour of the city and we were received at the reading with warmth and generosity. I was swept up to meet Murphy and other Dublin luminaries, with flattering introductions from Dennis. He seemed to be claiming me as some kind of expert on Irish poetry; but while Murphy's *The Battle of Aughrim* sang in our ears, there was the feeling that, different as we children of the fifties were, we had both left a High Island and were meeting – English poet, Irish poet – on a new, more low-lying spot. After this, whenever I was in Dublin, Dennis and I would try and have lunch together. There was never enough time, because we both had day-jobs, (those post-Yeatsian "responsibilities" of earning a living, attending to family), but that probably intensified the fellow-feeling. I look back sadly at those talk-filled, poem-crowded lunch-hours in the age of 'the Celtic Tiger' (another O'Driscoll theme), too few of them "snatched", as Dennis put it, "from the jaws of Customs". Knowing I was on a school-teacher's salary, he would insist on paying, though I would have drawn on my savings just to hear him talk. I remember at our last meeting how he dropped hints that something was brewing with his old friend Seamus Heaney, who was just recovering from a stroke – and it was going to be a major project. I felt privileged to have been let in on the secret.

What Dennis never suggested was that he himself was in poor health, that he might expect to die before he had reached sixty (as both of his parents had). In fact, I did not see him again after *Stepping Stones* appeared, when he was caught up in the promotional torrent and seemed to be fighting the swell of his own success (one of his letters mentions "five hundred plus poetry books" he had to assess for the prestigious Griffin Prize). Our school trips to Dublin fizzled out as the exchange rates worsened and the recession began; my only trip to Ireland thereafter was to Sligo and Coole Park – another world. Nor did my friend ever visit us in Huntingdonshire. But when in 2010 I encountered Seamus Heaney himself at Little Gidding – just a cycle-ride from our cottage – the conversation was almost entirely about Dennis, his remarkable personal qualities and his central role in Irish literature.

A few days before Christmas I received a card from Dennis and Julie. In the familiar bold, black hand, along with best wishes for the season, there was one sentence: "to John, looking forward hugely to your new book". He will not read it. But we will surely go on reading and re-reading his *Kist, Hidden Extras, Long Story Short, The Bottom Line, Quality Time, Weather Permitting, Exemplary Damages, Reality Check* and – from just last year, titled with poignant exactitude – his *Dear Life*.

John Greening recently received a Cholmondeley Award; his collection *To the War Poets* will appear from Carcanet this autumn. His Hawthornden sequence, *Knots*, is out from Worpel in April.

ℬ

REVIEWS

❧

...having an elephant for a consort has the
advantages [...] of no conversation and no sex

– *Carrie Etter*

Under the Purple Grapes

SUSAN WICKS

Ko Un, *First Person Sorrowful*, trans. Brother Anthony of Taizé
and Lee Sang-Wha, Bloodaxe, £9.95, ISBN 9781852249533;
Ali Alizadeh and John Kinsella (eds. and trans.), *Six Vowels & Twenty-three
Consonants: An Anthology of Persian Poetry from Rudaki to Langroodi*,
Arc, £11.99, ISBN 9781906570576;
David Harsent, *In Secret: Versions of Yannis Ritsos*, Enitharmon,
£9.99, ISBN 9781907587214.

As Martha Kapos pointed out in a recent editorial of *Poetry London*, the UK has seen an explosion of translated poetry in recent years. Since the Eastern European discoveries of the nineteen sixties and nineties, our poetic horizons have been forcibly widened, leading us to interrogate not just our own 'native' poetic tradition, but also our openness and versatility as readers. With poems in translation, familiar ways of reading may not be enough. However accomplished the translator, we aren't often beguiled in quite the same way: the rhythms are inevitably that much prosier, the conceptual leaps starker, the palette of imagery subtly different from our own. We find ourselves asking not just *what* we are reading, but why. Are we reading for knowledge, as students of a foreign culture or ideological landscape, where the gratifications we normally expect of poetry are incidental? Or are we truly hoping to be surprised and delighted in ways that are all the more delightful and surprising for not being our own? Reading these three very different books, I found I was at times a student, at times a cultural traveller, at times both or neither.

Whatever our origins, it would be hard to wrap our minds round the life experiences of the Korean poet Ko Un. A human rights activist, a former Buddhist monk, traumatised by war and repeated imprisonment, the author of more than one hundred and fifty volumes of poetry, essays and fiction, he seems to defy the eloquence even of Andrew Motion's persuasive introduction to this first UK selection. But open *First Person Sorrowful* at almost any page and Ko Un himself is there to help: "I was an egg broken / before it became a chick [...]". If we can only forget what we thought we knew about the sublime of mountain landscapes, about anthropomorphism and the pathetic fallacy, we find ourselves entering a poetry in which mountains can be small and rivers sorrowful, where the individual is both dwarfed and elevated:

> I let my ridiculous white pages fly away.
> I write with my body alone,
> with my soul alone.
> I write in the empty sky.

The ambitions of this poetry are at the same time humble and huge. Ko Un's work is the work of a whole person, as alive to current conflicts in Kabul as it is to Homer or *The Mahabharata* or Mallarmé's white page. It can even accommodate humour. Ko's voice, in Brother Anthony and Lee Sang-Wha's unshowy translation, urges us to take that step into the unknown:

> Oh, the many thousands of years contained in a word!
> A friend who will change my face is coming, flying
> from the unknown like the cries of white gulls.

In *Six Vowels and Twenty-Three Consonants* we are in danger of thinking ourselves in more familiar territory – but any lingering half-memories of the nineteenth century translator Edward FitzGerald are soon seen for the misleading signposts they are. This is at the same time a very beautiful and a very useful anthology. Two impeccably written and documented introductions by co-translator Ali Alizardeh give historical and current political context and a welcome unifying perspective to poets and poems caught between shifting nations, faiths and boundaries. Yet, across the thirteen centuries spanned by this selection, a Persian linguistic and poetic tradition is recognisable, embracing well-known figures such as Omar Khayyam and Rumi while subtly challenging our previous uncontextualised Western readings. This book has great integrity. Students and scholars will welcome the linkages it makes possible, not least its acknowledgement of an important strand of energetic writing and experimentation among women poets. But everyone will surely relish the design and layout of this book. In this poetry, where, in Rumi's words, "All life is held by those who have let their cacophony die", white space itself is particularly important, and the publishers have had the sense to see this. The whole book is an acknowledgement that we read poems differently according to how and where they reach us. There are formal echoes – couplets, quatrains, ghazals. There are recurring themes and images – sexual desire, wine, ships, bloodshed. But while the book's documentation seems to ask us to to read as students, its uncluttered design allows us to read as lovers of poetry too. In the words of its youngest poet, Ahmad Zahedi Langroodi:

> The flower in the rug's
> geometrical rhythm repeats
> and when it touches the foot
> the small girl has become a bride.

It's easy to see the attraction for David Harsent of Yannis Ritsos's poetry. The short disturbing narratives that open *In Secret* have the urgent logic of dreams, their roots visibly in historical reality, their gaps the universal human gaps of incomprehension and anxiety. We find ourselves asking, *Who?*, *Where?*, *When?* and, like dreams, the unattached stories give rise to a queasy sense of displacement. The title poem moves in six lines from illuminated ship to picture hat to scaffold – real or allegorical? – while we blink. In other poems, 'Penelope', for instance, the fragment from 'Agamemnon' or the powerful 'The Crane Dance', Ritsos inhabits the myth so completely it seems actual. We're in the presence of a mind as at home with fragmentation as it is with sequential narrative, where the ordinary objects and rituals of daily existence reveal their inherent strangeness. This poetry is fascinating for what it seems to leave out – "like that knife there, hidden / under the grapes. Under the purple grapes."

And all this comes to us, it seems, without linguistic barriers. *In Secret* is presented as "versions". In his low-key afterword David Harsent makes no claim to translating these poems from the originals – or even, as far as I could see, to any knowledge of modern Greek at all. But the fact is that the sureness and versatility of his poetic ear and vocabulary free us to experience the deeper structures of Ritsos's poetry apparently without intermediary, and the experience is exhilarating. The atmosphere of political upheaval and threat of violence are as present here as in the Ko Un. And here the language seems to put us into dialogue with them directly. We hardly need even our sunglasses or our torch.

Susan Wicks's translation of Valérie Rouzeau's *Pas Revoir* as *Cold Spring in Winter* (Arc 2009) was shortlisted for the International Griffin Prize for Poetry and won the Scott-Moncrieff Prize. Valérie Rouzeau's latest collection, *Vrouz* (La Table Ronde, 2012) recently won the Apollinaire Prize.

℘

An Ear for Murmurs

ZOË BRIGLEY

Menna Elfyn, *Murmur* (Welsh-English Bilingual Edition),
Bloodaxe, £9.95, ISBN 9781852249441;
Gillian Clarke, *Ice*, Carcanet, £9.95, ISBN 9781847771995.

Menna Elfyn's elegant new collection, *Murmur*, takes its title from Rainer Maria Rilke's *Sonnets to Orpheus*. The epigraph quotes 'Sonnet XXIX', where Rilke demands that if mortals can no longer name the divine, then it must "Murmur to the quiet earth: I flow, / Voice to the running water: I exist". The act of listening is significant and Elfyn plays on the double meaning of "murmur" in Welsh; the English and Welsh word for "murmur" are the same, but "mur" is also the Welsh word for wall. Breaking down the barriers between human beings is often the subject matter of Elfyn's poems, and in 'Ghazal Colli' ('Ghazal: Loss'), she plays on the chiming between "murmur" and "marmor" (the Welsh word for marble). Yet the title poem suggests that walls can be generative and protective too: "waliau yw seiniau / yr heniaith" ("walls are sounds / of the old tongue"). Elfyn's discussion of human relations is bound up with her status as a Welsh-speaking poet: "yr heniaith" meaning Cymraeg (the Welsh language). Her fear is that Cymraeg will be marred by shibboleth, becoming merely a "language of silence" read on the page.

This version of *Murmur*, published by Bloodaxe, features English translations of Elfyn's poems in Cymraeg. The translators are a dream-team of Welsh writers: Joseph P. Clancy, Gillian Clarke, Damian Walford Davies, Paul Henry and Elinor ap Hywel. The translations, however, rarely remain totally faithful to the original poems and I suspect that this is deliberate on Elfyn's part. Certainly, each poet is allowed to bring a different kind of phrasing and form to Elfyn's poetry, and there are secrets and nuances to be uncovered in the originals by speakers of Cymraeg. *Murmur* also displays Elfyn's own skill in translation, as she presents some fine versions of Welsh-language poet Waldo Williams and of her own sequence for Catrin Glyndŵr.

Owain Glyndŵr, who led the fifteenth century Welsh Revolt against Henry IV, had a daughter, Catrin. Though her father evaded capture, Catrin and her daughters were taken to the Tower of London where they were mysteriously killed. Elfyn presents a moving account of a mother trying to protect her children from grim reality. In 'Siôl' ('Shawl'), Catrin escapes her prison walls through the act of breastfeeding:

> Trois fy sioˆl yn gynefin.
> Am yn ail eu magu
> ar ysgwydd, mewn coˆl,
> ar y fron, eu rhwymo'n dynn.
>
> I made of my shawl a home.
> One by one I nursed them,
> against my shoulder, on my lap,
> at the breast, wrapped them close.

These moments are precious but futile; the children are taken away, never to be seen again.

Such murmurs from history echo into the present. Elfyn recalls the story of Mynydd Epynt in Mid-Wales where a Welsh-speaking community was expelled so that the army could perform military drills on the mountain. 'Murmur' links this act of violence on Welsh communities to wars in the Middle East. An army officer on Epynt tells how he takes off his shoes as a gesture of respect on entering an Afghanistan abode. Elfyn wryly adds "ar ôl cicio'r drws i mewn" ("after kicking the door down"). Commenting on the barbarity of the imperialist mindset, she echoes Waldo Williams's words in her translation of his poem 'Pa Beth Yw Dyn?' (translated as 'To Live'): "What's the world to the all powerful? / A circle spinning. / And to the children of the earth? / A cradle rocking."

If Elfyn seeks to highlight murmurs of protest, Gillian Clarke also is interested in finding spaces where listening is possible. Clarke's superb new collection, *Ice*, nominated for the T.S. Eliot Prize, exists in the blankness and silence of winter snow. 'Ice Music' portrays a couple at opposite ends of the country, both hearing "a moan of expanding ice / a timpani of plates colliding, a cry of icicles". The act of listening is political too, since Clarke records sounds of pain that we try to ignore in the West: the cry of a widow in Afghanistan who "crouches in the rubble / over a son, a brother torn apart"('Listen') and "the cry of the earth as it broke its heart" ('Lament for Haiti').

Clarke's poems are indeed painful. They describe the cold and barrenness of winter, and the suffering of birds – swans, wrens and grebes. This extends too into bleak human subjects: the murder of a girl found dead by the side of the road in 'Freeze 2010' and the suffering of the elderly: "The old in city flats found three months dead" ('The Dead after the Thaw'). Winter's deadliness is encapsulated by the figure of Marged who is mentioned in a number of poems; a previous tenant of Clarke's house during the 1930s, Marged committed suicide in the depths of winter.

By examining the bleakest season of the year, Clarke is able to uncover disturbing themes, including coming to terms with loss. The opening poem, 'Polar', laments the endangered status of the polar bear, affirming "I want him alive. / I want him fierce". What is lost, however, is gone forever: "had they not shot the bear, / had they not loosed the ice, / had not, had not..."

'River' flows over "the brimming ribcage / of a drowned beast" and, in 'Freeze 1947', the narrator imagines that the "polar bear rug on the living room floor / rose from the dead, shook snow from its fur". Clarke's poetry seeks to recapture the essence of things passed. Her lost Welsh tongue. Her long dead grandparents. A memory from childhood of boarding a ship on Cardiff docks. A fleeting rainbow on Llanberis Pass.

Ice has intriguing connections, too, to Clarke's body of work. She returns to familiar themes – the birthing of lambs and the five fields of her home. Water, the lifeforce for much of her poetry, returns, though it is transformed by the frost. The deathliness of winter gives Clarke's poetry a fresh urgency. Her narrators are all too aware of the painful process of decline, yet they celebrate too the beauty of things passing. In 'Blue Hydrangeas', the narrator compares the deterioration of flowers to her mother's aged skin, and now her own.

> You found them, lovely, silky, dangerous,
> their lapis lazulis, their indigos
> tidemarked and freckled with the rose
>
> of death, beautiful in decline.
> I touch my mother's skin. Touch mine.

The command at the end of the poem turns the scrutiny from an aged parent to the narrator herself who takes her mother's place. Though aged, the speaker is still "lovely, silky, dangerous" like the hydrangeas. The narrators of Clarke's poems are not helpless or maudlin as they contemplate the painfulness of decline, but they do face the raw, inevitable pain of life as something to be revelled in. *Ice* rightly entreats its readers to value what Clarke describes in 'This Year's Midnight' as "the fallen, / the golden ones", because their knowledge may have something to contribute to a deteriorating world: "Listen! They are whispering / now while the world talks, / and the ice melts, / and the seas rise."

Zoë Brigley's most recent poetry collection *Conquest* (Bloodaxe, 2012) was a Poetry Book Society Recommendation.

ZB

Raw Souls

ERIK MARTINY

Sharon Olds, *Stag's Leap*, Cape, £10, ISBN 9780224096942;
Jorie Graham, *PLACE*, Carcanet, £9.95, ISBN 9781847771933.

Opening one of Olds's collections can make you feel as if you're about to unearth a time capsule from the underground heartland of poetry itself, for, although each poem strikes you with fresh force, most of Olds's collections are about ten years in the making. There have been hints that marital breakup was to become a major subject for Olds since *The Unswept Room* (Cape, 2003), but this is the first collection that brings you face to face with all the "courtesy and horror" of divorce.

Stag's Leap is so deft and intense that it bears easy comparison with the narrative thrust and thrill dispensed by her finest collections. The sense that the world of letters has been given the godsend of another collection that matters deeply, grows on you with every passing page.

Olds's use of lineation can be as sharp as a cliffhanger sentence in a thriller, despite the fact that the actions described are the protracted moments before a husband leaves his wife: "He bears his bony tray / level as he soars from the precipice edge, / dreamy. When anyone escapes, my heart / leaps up. Even when it's I who am escaped from, / I am half on the side of the leaver."

These are lines from the start of the title poem 'Stag's Leap' which evoke the drawing of a stag on the label of the erstwhile couple's favourite wine. As in all of her work, it is the masterful metaphors that obtain the most riveting effects. Even in very short lyrics such as 'The Healers', a final image casts the poem into solid bronze, ensuring that it remains memorable. The poem, which begins by evoking the speaker's former sense of pride when her doctor husband was called on to help in airplanes, takes the emotional leap of imagining him with his new companion as equals, and then steers clear of such selfless grandeur by returning to the creative hardiness of her earlier work: "Oh well. It was the way / it was, he did not feel happy when words / were called for, and I stood" ('The Healers'). The beauty and dignity of her language have, from the start, given Sharon Olds's poems a strong aura.

The tone is beautifully balanced here and this is one of the successes of the collection: the ability to shift from one attitude to another without always settling for equanimity, even if this is the tone one is wont to admire in her work. Some of her new poems depart from her usual magnanimity, indulging in elegant flights of anger: 'Material Ode' draws on the miniature epic manner of some of her most salient, early, Whitman-inspired poems, with their tongue-in-cheek magniloquence:

> O tulle, O taffeta, O grosgrain –
> I call upon you now, girls,
> of fabrics and the woman I sing. My husband
> had said he was probably going to leave me – not
> for sure, but likely maybe – and no, it did not
> have to do with her. O satin, O
> sateen, O velvet, O fucking velveeta –
> the day of the doctors' dress-up dance,
> the annual folderol, the lace,
> the net, he said it would be hard for her
> to see me there, dancing with him,
> would I mind not going.

There's a fine line between satin and Sharon Olds's early Satan figure in these imprecations. They possess the delicacy of Emily Dickinson's "tippet only tulle" stretched out on tenterhooks.

Jorie Graham's latest collection of poems, soberly entitled *PLACE*, offers the reader a very different aesthetic experience. To begin with, there is little sense of interpersonal communion in Graham's collection: whereas Olds's poems are invariably focused on human relationships, Graham's lyrics tend to record the "atoms as they fall", to quote Virginia Woolf's phrase. The ideal time of day for registering these earth-bound sensations is frequently morning. Graham has written aubades before, poems in which the traditional idea of a lover wooing through music is, however, generally absent. Graham's morning songs are usually mournful. And the atmosphere is not always bucolic. Her version of the Larkinesque aubade is darker because what Philip Larkin mostly loathed was death; the speaker of Graham's poem 'Waking' is not weary of the "rented world" but of nature too and of the life one knows: "To be one who has had / enough. Enough of the basement. / Enough of the garden / with its high wall".

More than a few of Graham's wandering lines seem to roam around in search of oblivion, an escape from the sometimes nightmarish dream sequences the speaker seems to inhabit (her use of lineation creates a regularity of blank space on the page as well): "I will put into you this distance spiked with gigantic summits I can't handle any more, / a place neither childhood nor future fill, a self-erasing page". These are the monologues of a grounded cosmonaut exploring what the late J.G. Ballard liked to call "inner space".

'Treadmill' is one of the finer poems in the collection, charting the trajectory of a consciousness from feelings of existentially claustrophobic entrapment ("our skulled-in mind") to sensations of release from limitation ("you / feel your astonishing aloneness grow funnily / winged"). What is exciting about Graham's work is the expectation that anything can happen. There is nothing comfortable or staid about the surrealist experiences recounted in this and other poems. Her most powerful effects are achieved through the effective use of deliberately inappropriate word combinations and surprisingly frequent personifications, which sometimes recall Sylvia Plath's recourse to the trope: "have you not looked into them enough says the grayish / road, hissing, or maybe / that is my mind, I / entered the poem here, / on line 28, at 6:44 pm, I had been trying to stay outside, I had not wanted to / put my feet here too".

The main thing to avoid with these two collections is reading them consecutively. The thrust and parry of Sharon Olds's incisive lines, and that sense of what Peter Redgrove called her "solid reality", can make Jorie Graham's metaphysical questionings seem like watered-down Beckett. Graham's complex crystals should ideally be appraised after having abstained from reading anything for a week.

Erik Martiny's reviews have appeared in the *TLS* and *The London Magazine*; he also writes on contemporary art for *Fjords Review* and *Frieze Magazine*.

Positive Capabilities

CAROL RUMENS

Anne Stevenson, *Astonishment*, Bloodaxe, £8.95, ISBN 9781852249472;
Gerard Woodward, *The Seacunny*, Picador, £9.99, ISBN 9781447217428.

The biggish bang of Modernism goes on sparking off littler bangs. There must be dozens of poetic universes in the UK alone – centres and off-centres of fashion, delegations from all strongholds of identity-politics, and the literary equivalents of atonal and diatonic composition in music, with every brow-height in between. Sometimes the differences are fewer than we think. But differences there are, and it's interesting to compare two poets who are seemingly worlds apart.

In 'Constable's Clouds and a Kestrel Feather', Anne Stevenson's speaker, after purposefully playing "the cloud-zoo game," abandons cloud-fancying to view the symmetry of a kestrel's feather. She deduces that "Nature's nature is to work from form" – questionable as an observation about clouds, but clearly pointing to Stevenson's own desire to shape what she sees. Gerard Woodward's 'Cow Tipping' suggests more of a boyish prank. After some thoughtful, naturalistic observation down among the cattle, he wonders about poking them with one finger, so they spill "like dominoes", then extricates himself from the possibly pointless exercise: "Forget it. And none of this is true anyway." Neither poem is the author's greatest hit, but both are illustrative. From their titles (a lesson taught to art by nature for Stevenson, a daft experiment for Woodward), to their slightly faux conclusions, both declare an ars poetica – of organised mimesis and artful subversion, respectively.

Woodward is a careful poet who delights in the game of language. He is also an excellent reporter, with an almost 'Martian' way of making the ordinary not only strange, but strangely recognisable. His speakers never wholly trust transcendence. Stevenson values transcendence if she can honestly earn it. Woodward has his finger not only on the cows but also on the zeitgeist: he shares the art of the tall story and its deeper questioning with Irish and Irish-influenced poets such as Matthew Sweeney, Paul Muldoon, Ian Duhig and Jo Shapcott. Stevenson belongs to a more confident generation of truth-seekers and values the poet-as-teacher. In form, she's a melodist; Woodward, though never slack, is less 'bel canto'.

Stevenson's debt to American transcendentalism is signalled in

'Teaching My Sons to Swim in Walden Pond', with its epigraph from Thoreau: "We must look a long time before we can see." The poem is elegantly shaped, with indented lines to emphasise the cadences. The subject invites a certain bossiness ("Pooh! Everything to do with learning hurts") but the poem evolves into something more mysterious, closer to Frost in tone as well as imagery: "What if – at some road fork in evolution – / we'd taken instead the dolphin's way? / The seal's, the otter's? We need to swim / to keep that lost road open."

Clear vision cohabits with the visionary. She identifies with "the poet-scientist" in the above poem, and her imaginative long view of human history is part of a search for principles to unify the inter-disciplinary strands of human enquiry. But opinion can block the way. Less than dispassionate as she reviews "the infallible i of the pad, the pod, the impudent phone," the speaker in 'Online' seems certain that the new technology costs the young their "Independence" and makes everyone self-centred. The disapproval is feisty, but the scientist-philosopher-poet might interestingly enquire further. Despite the collection's title (from Derek Walcott's "The perpetual ideal is astonishment"), and some luminous moments of spring-awakening, the most resonant mood is a wry sadness. See, for instance, 'An Exchange in the Time Bank', a coolly told parable in which a senior Life Insurance policy-holder asks what she has earned in "retrievable memories" and is chillingly informed "it's not possible / for post-seventies savings grants to be guaranteed." Balance is Stevenson's key skill, a matter of emotional intelligence as well as craft. Her achievements include 'Photographing Change', 'Demeter's Daughter', 'Spring Again', 'A Visit' (a lovely, casual-seeming elegy) and, my favourite of a series of graceful sonnets, 'Caring More Than Caring'. Negative capability here becomes a virtue in human relations as well as muse-courtship: "My not visiting, your not wanting me – / What could bring us closer to understanding / The unsaid rules of truth in poetry?"

For Woodward "the truth in poetry" seems founded on the laws and bizarre anti-laws of physics. His detailed reports on trampolining, archery and electricity, for example, show an easy assimilation of scientific concepts to keen, naked-eyed, empathetic observation. He is rarely tempted by the concluding moral: in fact, he has made something of an art of the comic shrug. Sometimes, the occasion for the poem seems a slight one, or a little too carefully set up, but usually Woodward's world- and word-relishing charm saves the day. He builds steady increments of bizarreness in the title-poem – about moving a bird-table increasing distances from the house to "bring the birds joyously / to this little chalet on a pole [...]". The visitor who finally arrives is the Seacunny – a name which sounds like a bird, but means, in Laskari dialect, an Indian sailing-ship navigator. Never mind: this seacunny is only a pretend-bird (child-made, perhaps), "Dressed in a smock of glue and feathers, with a plastic / Cup dabbed yellow for a beak [...]". While some of the poems hint at a private joke, they twinkle expansively enough to include the reader, and a sharp, competitive performance never forgets the 'Caring More Than Caring' tenderness of detail.

Woodward's poems are often seriously funny, with that touch of nihilism all true comedy has. His style might be generalised as the domestic post-modern, provided you remember to laugh at the very idea. Stevenson's work, taking form and colouration from its ambience, is resistant to categorisation. More complex than the opinions it releases, her candour inspires trust. She can surely say of her poems, as she has Rembrandt say of his paintings, "My pictures, whatever my will, / told the truth to my eyes!"

Carol Rumens's most recent collection of poems, *De Chirico's Threads*, was published by Seren in 2010.

℘

Something Indeed

JOHN GREENING

Andrew Motion, *The Customs House*, Faber, £12.99, ISBN 9780571288108;
Jamie McKendrick, *Out There*, Faber, £9.99, ISBN 9780571289110;
Angela Leighton, *The Messages*, Shoestring, £9, ISBN 9781907356308.

Having already enjoyed the Clutag chapbook, *Laurels and Donkeys*, which essentially makes up the first part of Andrew Motion's collection, your reviewer began with Part 2, 'The Exploration of Space', poems which launch themselves on the air, their main verbs frequently held back ("When you stepped...', 'Remembering how...") or darting forward deceptively ("The hare we disturbed in the yard of Home Farm, / that either limped ahead of us or..."). It is a very Edward Thomas-ish way of writing, the sentence carrying us downhill, or along a path to see some fallen petals. Motion knows full well what his influences are, even gently encoding

Thomas's phraseology, for example, in the first of his skeletal bird poems ("Of All the Birds [...] The magpie I like least..."). But what is interesting is that this new stylistic openness reflects something chillier than usual in the poems themselves, as if Motion had taken us through his other master's high windows. It is presumably "unresting death", one collection nearer now. As so often before, Motion's mother is remembered, and increasingly his father. The shade of Mick Imlah ("as I knew you then") visits him. And he again commemorates Larkin (differently from 'This is your subject speaking') in a poem which slightly misquotes 'The Whitsun Weddings' – just one of the deliberately unsettling aspects to *The Customs House*.

Something of the same cool, bright aesthetic informs the tribute to his teacher, Peter Way, whose importance Motion has acknowledged elsewhere. His schoolboy awakening to poetry is set beside the discovery of a "forgotten treasure of test-tubes and pipettes", which he thinks of as "the remains of a glass child" – not realising that he is making metaphors. Perhaps all good poems are really about poetry itself. Motion's solitary singer of the wastes in the final sequence, 'Whale Music', could be a poet, just as his Customs House (or is it Larkin's?) could be poetry.

But for all the authority in these and in the opening remembrances – the found poems, the tribute to Harry Patch, the exploration of the confusion of battle as experienced and as recalled ('In Normandy') – the heart of *The Customs House* is 'The Death of Francesco Borromini'. Intended to accompany the seventh of Peter Maxwell Davies's astonishing 'Naxos' Quartets, 'Metafore sul Borromini', a vast work in seven slow movements, each of which is shadowed here, Motion's sequence elaborates on ideas in and behind the music, even incorporating Maxwell Davies's own diary notes (how he spotted a pair of ballet shoes left at the architect's tomb, for example). There is a pervasive sense of light dancing, of the poet shaping something from the very air, as composers do, as the architect himself did, understanding "the weight of stone is the same as the weight of air / and, like a breeze blowing across a field of wheat, / will sway, curve, vault, bow, spin, stop and stand / with a visible force and leave the clear impression / of things by nature continually unseen and invisible..."

At first, Jamie McKendrick seems to be heading through the same (albeit sonnet-shaped) windows, noting in 'Out There' –

> What once had been
> where heaven was, is barren beyond imagining,
> and never so keenly as from out there can
> the lost feel earth's the only paradise.

But his "indefinite zone" is not entirely devoid of spirit; we encounter fall, flood, hell, judgement, lepers, priests, fishers of men, a crown of thorns, a Meeting House and indeed a Buddha. It's all done in the best, modern way, of course – the comforting clutter of "the lost". 'The Possessors' is a meditation on how "the only things that animals possess / apart from parasites, are what they hold / between their teeth" and on how the poet has become "like an overburdened camel / wedged in the strait gate of Jerusalem". Fond of the visual arts (his has long been the verse of the collector as well as the dreamer and thinker), McKendrick inclines to interpret nature like a painting. So, the moon is a "chiaroscuro" that might "start to pall" if it were closer. In fact, as the book's title suggests, he is rather intrigued by distance, by the inaccessible – Uranus, a far-off oak, a violin he can't play, a vanished moment of intense blueness ('Azurite'). But this poet is not easily pinned down. 'Epithets' is about his native Liverpool; 'King Billy's Nemesis' deals with moles. A natural elegist (again Mick Imlah is commemorated; so is the art critic Tom Lubbock), McKendrick can nevertheless be very funny. I would not have missed his 'Stricken Proverbs' ("A rip in space needs a stitch in time", "Time's flies wait to feast on no man") nor his quirky, anaphoric 'Fly Inventory'. And 'Guilt', about dreaming he had killed a poet after "an involuntary expression of disdain / and the absence of a single word of praise", prompts me both to admire this collection and to move on.

As daughter of the composer Kenneth Leighton it is not surprising that Angela Leighton writes poems that often feature, allude to or aspire to the condition of music. "Owls' oboes, duo, their wit and hoo...", one begins. Titles include 'Kite in 4.4 time', 'Busking' and 'For the End of Time'. There is a scallop for Britten and a chanterelle for Robin Holloway. Curiously, Leighton devotes a poem to the same 'Wolf note' (the jarring sound a stringed instrument can make when its body resonates) that sounds twice at the end of McKendrick's collection. He found himself "attuned" to it, but she tries to play it in the very lines of her verse:

> You can put your finger on it, feel
> a fault in the line, pleat under pressing,
>
> a cross, locked in the logic of it,
> imp in the works, glitch in the ribbing...

Hers is a denser, more instinctively alliterative, less fashionable style than the urbane conversation pieces of Motion and McKendrick, yet the pleasures to be found here are as intense as the poems. Topics range beyond music into art of all kinds but draw repeatedly on nature. A gekko is "a sudden comma commandeered by feet"; hoar frost –

> A crinkling cold   electric silver shot
> white bones exposed
>   hot stuff   but biting
> pricked on the windward side
>   ('Three Shorts: Winter')

Leighton picks her way, clause by phrase, seeking the surest word or image, as if she were crossing the Fens around Tennyson's Trinity, where she is based. If lines such as "What do they see, the far-sighted dreamers, / readers, sight-seers / of the sea's blue moveable script...?" taste of the Lotos, more often their many-faceted clarity recalls *In Memoriam*, a work she commemorates here. Another poem, 'Ammonite', ghosts Tennyson's famous stanza even as it raises Lyell and Darwin: "Who knocks so hard? Safe and shut / the rock's sarcophagus, chipped door / of earth's unfathomably packed store. / No way back. You hammer and scratch. // Then something..."   Something indeed. Angela Leighton should be on anyone's list of essential poets.

John Greening recently received a Cholmondeley Award; his collection *To the War Poets* will appear from Carcanet this autumn. His Hawthornden sequence, *Knots*, is out from Worpel in April.

ℬ

T.S. ELIOT INTERNATIONAL SUMMER SCHOOL
6-14 July 2013

The Institute of English Studies is hosting the fifth annual T.S. Eliot International Summer School. Poetry lovers and Eliot enthusiasts are invited to this week-long celebration of the life and writing of one of the greatest modern English poets. The summer school offers lectures and seminars, social evenings, excursions to Burnt Norton, Little Gidding and East Coker, and a poetry reading by Christopher Reid, winner of the 2009 Costa Book of the Year Award.

For enquiries, registration and programme information:
http://ies.sas.ac.uk | Tel: +44 (0)20 7862-8680
E-mail: iesevents@sas.ac.uk | Twitter: @IESLondon

INSTITUTE OF ENGLISH STUDIES | School of Advanced Study
University of London

Rain from a Once-Only Sky

HELEN MORT

Penelope Shuttle, *Unsent: New & Selected Poems 1980-2012,*
Bloodaxe, £12, ISBN 9781852249502.

> Let cloud work out what to do with Kynance.
> Let the rain select its own towns.
> Let the untaught waterfalls solve
> the traffic problems of Wadebridge...

'A Future for Cornwall', from Penelope Shuttle's 1999 collection *A Leaf Out of His Book*, imagines a world where the natural order reclaims our towns: while "all the windows close on Truro" ... "spiders overtake Redruth". Twelve years on, Shuttle's poem seems prescient, but its vision of a world in which nature asserting its power over human settlements is a restoration, rather than an imposition, is particularly refreshing.

Climate change has shifted the way writers think about the planet and our relationship to it. We are not living in the Holocene any more. We're living in the Anthropocene – a phase of geological time fundamentally shaped by humans. The role that poetry might play in this new epoch is unclear - reject the idea of 'nature' entirely, since we seem so abstracted from it? Write only about environmental themes, as the pressing issues of the day? Try to recreate the concept of the sublime? Penelope Shuttle's collected work, written over more than three decades, suggests a different way of approaching these themes: in her poems, the idea of 'nature' itself is redundant, since that implies a division between us and the world, a divide that does not really exist.

Since the 1970s, Shuttle has pioneered an original, sensuous approach to writing her way into and out of landscapes, merging the elemental and the personal, her work influenced more by European writers such as Lorca, Rilke and Akhmatova than by the British poets who were writing at the time. In her poetry and in prose such as *The Wise Wound* (1978), written with her husband Peter Redgrove, she suggests ways of looking at bodies and their environments which disregard traditional boundaries of intellectual enquiry. As the authors of *The Wise Wound* put it, this is work that always shows how "the polarisation between science and art is unnecessary and is likely to prove deadly... the creative process of discovery is the same process in both science and art". Shuttle's propensity to interrogate physical boundaries is highlighted in *Unsent*, drawing together a body of work which unites the intellectual and the physical with bold directness.

Her first collection, *The Orchard Upstairs* (1980), is a book of thin and translucent things – rain, the gaps between bones – epitomised by the poem 'Glass-maker', where the narrator longs to be transparent since "to make glass / is clearer communication than speech". Boundaries are flimsy. In 'Appletree in America', the landscape merges into "the familiar loam of everything", leaving the poet "unanchored at twilight". The poems that take inspiration from motherhood in Shuttle's first collection explore the idea of being a vessel for the outer world:

> Rain falls on gardens and inscriptions
> but I hold the edge of the rain.
> I am a receptacle
> in which other rain, amniotic, gathers,
> for the one in his official residence
> to enjoy.
>
> ('Expectant Mother')

There's something deliberately "unanchored" in the language here too – the image of the edge of rain seeming both invisible and real at the same time. In poems such as 'The Conceiving', we seem to see right through the mother's skin, as if she has achieved her wish to be glass.

In Shuttle's two subsequent collections, *The Child Stealer* (1983) and *The Lion from Rio* (1986), motherhood makes the world new and strange:

> But how can I describe
> the mastery of flowers
> grazing the earth,
>
> like translations done
> without dictionaries?
>
> ('Twilight')

The idea of translating without a dictionary seems an apt analogy for Shuttle's fluid language. There's a generous instinct at work here, too, captured by this notion of the poet unable to describe a world too vast to be reduced to phrase-making. Even though her poems are often earthy, fiercely embodied,

Shuttle has a gift for transmutation. *Adventures With My Horse* (1988) is alive with a sensitivity to the world of animals, from 'Jungian Cows', to 'Killiow Pigs' ("like ambitious rabbits, with their long carefree / strokeable backs, their feet comic and smooth"), from 'Draco, the Dreaming Snake', to the horse suggested in the book's title:

> He does not complain of my weight on his back
> any more than darkness complains of its loneliness.
>
> The horse who loves me
> wields the prick of pain that caps the dart of love.
>
> ('The Horse Who Loves Me')

Like the other human analogies in Shuttle's imagery, the idea of darkness being capable of complaint does not seem anthropocentric – in Shuttle's language, human bodies imitate the environment as much as animals and landscapes exhibit human characteristics. There's a hopeful kind of democracy at work in much of her imagery.

Even when Shuttle considers loss directly in a poem such as 'Thief' ("he comes like a pauper on a dark patchwork morning / when summer is turning round and robs you blind"), the prospect seems to make the narrator more alive to the preciousness of the world:

> He takes everything you have, this thief, but gives you one gift.
>
> Each morning you open your eyes jealous as hunger, you walk
> serpent-necked and dwarf-legged in the thief's distorting mirrors,
> you go nakedly through the skyless moonless gardens and pagodas
> of envy that he gives you, the thief's gift, your seeding wilderness.

Physical descriptions almost seem to trip over each other, tongue-twisting and strange. The idea of a "skyless" garden is extraordinary yet, typically, Shuttle manages to sneak this strangeness past the reader, presenting it as if it were as normal as "moonless". This poem, with its complex approach to loss, seems almost prophetic when read alongside *Redgrove's Wife* (2006), *Sandgrain and Hourglass* (2010) and her latest poems, *Unsent* (2012), which form a triptych of mourning for her late husband, Peter Redgrove. Even in the depths of grief, Shuttle is connected to the world around her, sensitive to it as she tries to come to terms with a landscape changed by her husband's passing. In 'In the

Kitchen', she laments "I am trying to love the world / back to normal". In the haunting 'Missing You' she fears that "I've forgotten everything / the sun and moon taught me". When it seems impossible to love the world, Shuttle succeeds, somehow:

> When you're so tired
> you can't bear the world,
>
> that's when you really begin to live [...]   ('The World')

The new poems in *Unsent* achieve a kind of distance, after the immediacy of *Redgrove's Wife* and *Sandgrain and Hourglass*. The narrator in 'Hospital Song', imagines being both within and outside her own body ("I'm [...] my own operating theatre"). She is the visitor, the patient in the next bed, "the hospital / sleepless all night":

> I'm my own heartbeat
> pounding on and on
> > *but why?*
> long after yours has stopped.

Later, in 'Heart Watch', the poem's narrator treats the organ as if it is a separate, natural thing to be observed ("all that year I watched my heart / like a hunter, a birder"). There's a quiet acceptance in the poem's liminality, the fact that the heart is "neither broken or mended". As in *Redgrove's Wife* and *Sandgrain and Hourglass*, the poems in *Unsent* capture the ultimate isolation of grief:

> When you watch your heart all the time
> you get tired and fearful,
> no one helps you, no one says
> > let me take over for a while.

'Day in London' accurately describes the peculiar solitude that exists in cities, in places where we are surrounded by other people. Each evocation of London is extraordinarily tender and Shuttle is as attuned to these urban landscapes as she is to the uniqueness of the rural world. The narrator walks to the city "hurrying to meet you / who will stand me up forever". Ultimately, even when the heart is broken, Shuttle can find humour in it. 'Hearts' is typical of Shuttle's concise wit. She asks

> What is it with poets and their hearts?
> They leave them in the oddest places.
> Such carelessness would shock the ancient Egyptians [...[

Shelley's body ash is in Rome, his heart in Bournemouth. Hardy's heart is supposedly in a biscuit tin in Stinsford, far from his body in Poets' Corner. Shuttle concludes: "poets shouldn't be trusted with hearts, especially their own". Yet, in the work gathered in this *New and Selected*, the reader feels as if Shuttle has trusted us with hers, a little, and that we reciprocate.

℥

Helen Mort has published two pamphlets with tall-lighthouse and her collection, *Division Street*, is forthcoming from Chatto & Windus.

The Scale of Things

CLARE POLLARD

Deryn Rees-Jones, *Burying the Wren*, Seren, £8.99, ISBN 9781854115768; Kathleen Jamie, *The Overhaul*, Picador, £9.99, ISBN 9781447202042.

It is common for contemporary lyric poetry to focus upon details – a breakfast egg, a wildflower in a crack. There is a sense that poetry is about a quality of attention – that by really looking, the greatest epiphanies can be found in the everyday. It is easy to see why such a strategy is seductive: it takes confidence to tackle big ideas and epic subjects, whereas writing about light through the kitchen window feels more manageable. For many, such a tactic also illustrates what poetry is for: it forces us to slow down and observe our lives more keenly.

When such poems are so common, though, there are new risks involved. Attention is not necessarily enough. It takes an original mind to reanimate objects deadened to cliché by familiarity. Some nouns (pebbles, types of apple, flocks of starlings) can feel exhausted, and wringing epiphanies from them leads to contrivance. It is possible for details – "the Roethkean 'small things' of the universe" as Deryn Rees-Jones's blurb calls them – to lead to a safe, trivial poetry.

In Rees-Jones's collection, *Burying the Wren*, this is thankfully not the case. Minor objects become charms to hold against a feral universe. They act as portals to dizzying vastness: a trilobite is a bullethole, a sacrament; slugs hold "midnight séances". In 'Shaved Fennel with Blood Oranges, Pomegranate, Pecorino', the meal, prepared as she hears of Thom Gunn's death on the radio, is: "food to take the winter out of all of us, / calling us as even now, / with its muscular flexing in foetal turns / I call my own child on" – it is summer, heat, joy, the impulse to life itself. Elsewhere, a peony becomes death as the speaker presses her face into it to "furnish it with whispers".

Mortality is everywhere. Poems circle the final months of Rees-Jones's husband, the writer Michael Murphy. Beauty is disturbing, out of kilter – a great white owl is "like the moon, missing its step in the sky". 'A Chinese Lacquer Egg' appears mysteriously in her hand, a delicate "unworded prayer", close to rapture but also like a tumour. In 'A Dream of Constellations', the deadly breeding of star-shaped "astrocytal cells" in the brain's darkness opens into a poem about the whole of the sky – an "untelling of the world" where the constellations unravel: "Ursa Minor became the headless bear [...] Sagittarius the archer, staggered, wounded, / ripped his arm on a jagged star". The poems of grief are unhinged and animal: "No one can love this horror, no one can want it," she says in the 'Dogwoman' sequence. "I'm crouched between my own thighs // With my dog heart and my dog soul."

The 'Burying the Wren' poems framing the book are particularly haunting. "I kissed you at the corner gate," Rees-Jones begins, as if in a folk-song. But the old tradition of parading a wren in a box in Ireland on St. Stephen's Day, asking for money to bury the wren, takes on a weird charge. The bird is both him and her – the cold, soft hairs behind his ears and her own fluttering breast, quick and dead; captive and wild. Like many of the tiny poems in this devastating collection it carries an almost unendurable weight – all of sex, life and death contained in its body.

Kathleen Jamie has been through numerous transformations in her career, most recently becoming an admired essayist with her collections of nature writing, *Findings* and *Sightlines*. Her publishers claim *The Overhaul* "broadens her poetic range considerably", but it seems to me that her current trajectory is not a broadening but a focusing inward – these are poems rooted in her local landscape, often pared to the barest elements.

This is exposing, both of Jamie's abundant talent and her weaknesses. At her best, these poems are pure concentration – 'Hawk and Shadow' feels inevitable as a scrap of an old song: "I watched a hawk / glide low across the hill, / her own dark shape / in her talons like a kill". 'An Avowal' sees bluebells with charming novelty – the wind teasing them because they nod yes to everything. I enjoyed the dark, fairytale qualities of 'The Wood' and 'Glamourie', and particularly loved the Scots versions of Hölderlin, which have a bracing vitality: "Bien wi yella pears, fu / o wild roses, the braes / fa intil the loch" ('Hauf o' Life').

Elsewhere though, looking has limits. 'The Study' has moonlight "stroking in mild concern / the telescope mounted / on its tripod, the books, / the attic stair". The speaker figures the moon as a prying intruder, politely ushering it onwards ("why query me? [...] Please, be on your way"), but it feels slight, the emotion a vehicle for the description (what poet really wishes the moon would disappear from view?). In 'The Roost' there is little original in the image of the rooks rising "from their stubble-fields", crying "kaah...kaah...kaah". They do, of course, but it isn't quite enough to make a satisfying new poem, even as Jamie gestures towards death. However sharply we watch, not every natural spectacle leads inevitably to a revelation. 'Doing Away' claims:

> Nowhere to go, nowhere I'd rather be
> than here, fulfilling my daily rituals.
>   Why would one want
> to absent oneself, when one's commute
>
> is a lonely hillside by-way, high
> above the river?

There is something in "one's commute" that distils my uncertainties about this collection – it strains for the universal in what is actually only personal. Jamie clearly experiences a deep sense of connectedness when she looks upon the stones and valleys of her world, but that does not mean that the reader necessarily will too. I am glad she has such an enviable commute, but for me the poems that work best in *The Overhaul* are those where her imagination leads us somewhere stranger.

Clare Pollard's latest book, *Ovid's Heroines*, will be published by Bloodaxe in May 2013.

ℬ

The Voices We Make

CARRIE ETTER

Jane Yeh, *The Ninjas*, Carcanet, £9.95, ISBN 9781847771476;
Sally Read, *The Day Hospital*, Bloodaxe, £8.95, ISBN 185224948X;
Selima Hill, *People Who Like Meatballs*, Bloodaxe, £9.95, ISBN 1852249455.

Jane Yeh's first collection, *Marabou* (Carcanet, 2005), showed her poetry in a relatively traditional light, with taut, historical dramatic monologues, capitalisations at the beginnings of lines, and lyrics on romantic relationships that avoid personal, potentially confessional detail. The only poem there suggestive of the changes to come in Yeh's second volume, *The Ninjas*, is another, decidedly different dramatic monologue, 'The Only Confirmed Cast Member Is Ook the Owl, Who Has Been Tapped To Play the Snowy White Owl Who Delivers Mail for Harry'. Here, Yeh's poetry is at its most playful – "Between takes, I did leg-lifts in my trailer" – and poignant: "My greatest talent is impersonation – / To simulate a person's idea of an owl".

While the capitalisations remain, the new book abounds in wit and invention, with far greater breadth and humour. The opening poem, 'After the Attack of the Crystalline Entity', boldly announces this trajectory, with its title from a *Star Trek: The Next Generation* episode and its speaker an android. *The Ninjas* is roughly divided between character studies, whether in third person or dramatic monologue, and ruminations on various subjects by a most contemporary speaker. The character studies include people in paintings, a stag, a panda and a jellyfish, while the ruminations or, perhaps, odes, cover the eponymous ninjas, kittens, witches and ghosts.

In many of the poems, Yeh employs her line in a new way. While in *Marabou* she often used short lines and punctuation to create a punchy rhythm, in this collection she obtains a similar effect with single-sentence lines that steadily shift perspective. Consider the opening stanza of 'The Birds':

> They pack up around three with their incessant chirping.
> Their headgear includes goggles, stripes, crests, and masks.
> They peck for a living for their grub, which sometimes includes grubs.
> They snack on gingerbread and candy corn from off witches' houses.

Admittedly, these single-sentence lines have a prosy feel, but as *The Ninjas* continues, the line's evocation of a distinctly contemporary mind-set and rhythm prove convincing.

While Yeh offers numerous dramatic monologues from unusually diverse characters, Sally Read's *The Day Hospital* gives voice to twelve "patients of The Day Hospital for the Elderly in Central London". We move from location to location over the course of a single day, making four stops: 8am in NW1, 10am (at presumably another locale) in NW1, 3pm in W1, and 5pm in N1. For each stop, Read provides a prose description of the local environment with its smells, sounds and sights, before making a note of each character's physical or psychological state.

Many of the elderly are immigrants – four Irish, one Polish, one Jamaican, two German, one Italian and one Russian, as well as two English; four are Jewish. Their diagnoses include Alzheimer's and schizophrenia, while others' remain uncertain. Given such combinations of illness, age and remove from their native countries, the monologues are predictably poignant; they derive their power, though, not only from their ability to create sympathy, but also from their vividness in depicting individual lives. In 'Bridget', the monologue of an elderly Irish woman with depression and agoraphobia who has not left her home for two years, Read deftly evokes that sense of enclosure through repetition:

> The light of the television set
>
> washes through me
>
> like a nip of Jameson's.
>
> The nip of Jameson's washes
>
> through me like a man's
>
> five o' clock shadow on my cheek.
>
> The man's shadow goes through me
>
> like a cold walk in winter fields.

In *People Who Like Meatballs*, a single speaker reigns for each of two sequences of poems that manifest Selima Hill's characteristic humour and wonderfully original analogies. Most poems consist of a single long sentence that, by using commas and semi-colons, can extend as long as fifty lines. In poems of six, or even sixteen, lines, this device gives the poem a greater sense of momentum. As the poems lengthen, though, the difficulty increases the further the poem travels from the opening declaration on which everything else depends; it becomes awkward, if not impossible, to keep the logic of the grammar and its meaning clear.

According to the blurb, the title sequence is about "a man's humiliation by a woman". While the speaker certainly desires to humiliate the man she addresses by constantly mocking him, the man seems less humiliated than abused and the speaker at times cringingly bitter. Yet what makes the sequence engaging is not the soured relationship but the alternative companion the speaker imagines for herself: an elephant. To put it most cynically, having an elephant for a consort has the advantages, for the speaker, of no conversation and no sex, but the animal's significance proves more nuanced. As the sequence progresses, the speaker exhibits increasing envy of the elephant's existence, especially its lack of a sophisticated consciousness, aware of neither time nor gymnastics. After disappointment in a romantic relationship and tangible self-dissatisfaction, the speaker finds, in the imagined companionship of an elephant, both comfort and ease.

The second and final sequence of the collection, 'Into My Mother's Snow-Encrusted Lap', presents another group of poems in which a speaker vilifies a single character, his mother. Here, though, the vulnerability of the child-self early in the sequence creates greater sympathy for him. These poems succeed most when working by indirection, as in this short poem:

The Pool

No one needs to know there is no pool,
no poolside bar, no guests who'll never know
it's nothing but a pool in a dream

where moonlit rubber ducks and drowned bees
that shimmer now because they shimmered then
circle in obedience to sorrow.

If throughout *People Who Like Meatballs* some poems seem decidedly more effective than others, that difference tends to lie in the poems' mode. Poems that catalogue accusations, however witty or fresh, essentially read like hearsay, while poems that evoke the speaker's feelings produce a richer sense of experience and understanding, suggesting, to offer just one example, what it may feel like to "be alone with an elephant / knee-deep in plantains and knee-deep in grace".

Carrie Etter is a poet, lecturer and critic.

Serious Play

JEM POSTER

Stephen Knight, *The Prince of Wails*, CB Editions, £7.99, ISBN 9780956735966;
Richard Price, *Small World*, Carcanet, £9.95, ISBN 9781847771582;
Jacob Polley, *The Havocs*, Picador, £9.99, ISBN 9781447207030.

'The Prince of Wails' was one of the soubriquets given to 1950s sob-singer Johnnie Ray, who is name-checked in Stephen Knight's new collection, along with a host of other cultural icons – the Ink Spots, Spider-Man, Harold Lloyd, Charlie Chaplin, Franz Kafka, Dr Who, Jim Reeves and Bob Hope, to mention just a few. This gathering of names is part of a wider tendency: a significant number of the poems in the collection are characterised by a free-wheeling eclecticism that sees an intrinsic value in the found object, and often seems content to present its various discoveries and observations in catalogue form, as in 'Thank You for Having Me':

> everyone's packing up everyone's going home
> the girl guides and the traffic wardens all the souls
> the neighbourhood has harboured downing placards
> turning signs like PUKKA PIES ... *they're delicious* CLOSED
> CLOSED EVERYTHING MUST GO the dummies stripped of clothes...

The apparent artlessness of such catalogues can, of course, be deceptive: 'Benthills Notebook' is probably not exactly what it purports to be, since its fragmentary observations ("cushions leaking foam. My shaver filling a metal bin. / The clocks put back") have been marshalled into rhyming couplets. Even the playful refusal to be bothered with the finer details of 'Thank You for Having Me' ("don't mourn them uselessly [*something something something*]" or "conquistadores / in tarnished [*technical term for piece of armour*]") is more artfully knowing than genuinely casual.

Playfulness of this kind functions as a counterweight to the profound sadness that informs a significant proportion of the poems. The shade of the poet's dead father haunts the collection: he's there as a silent revenant standing with the poet's daughter beside a garden pond in the volume's prefatory poem, while the final poem is a broken lament for the "gentle man [...] who could not stay a while". Even "the space where a door should have been" in the garage the poet's father refused to complete ('The Summer of Love') can be understood, in context, as indicative of a more grievous absence.

Richard Price's *Small World* is similarly preoccupied with mortality. The death of a friend is commemorated in the brief section 'In Memory', while the extended sequence that follows chronicles a loved one's life-threatening illness. The sequence offers a series of telling vignettes: the patient's inert body connected by pipes and wires to its support system; a fellow patient shouting for her false teeth; the flowers, banned from the ward, clogging up an annexe; the patient's eventual ride home in an outsourced ambulance. Carefully reticent, with an emphasis on observed detail and a marked (if faintly subversive) focus on the dispassionate discourse of the medical profession, the poems nevertheless carry a powerful emotional charge. There's grief here – at human vulnerability and the possibility of absolute loss – together with a deep undercurrent of love.

Grief and love combine, too, in the snapshots of family life that make up the bulk of the book's first section. Daughter Katie, wheelchair-bound and to some extent marginalised in the wider world beyond the family, occupies centre stage here, her lively, defiant personality emerging clearly from the small narratives in which she figures – racing through Tate Modern in her wheelchair or spitting her medication across the room, an "armchair dancer", strong from the waist up but unsupported by her frail feet. As its title suggests, the collection deals centrally with ideas of restricted or impeded life, but its own essential quality is an expansive compassion.

By far the most inventive and artistically ambitious of these three collections, Jacob Polley's *The Havocs* is a series of finely orchestrated variations on a number of related themes. The poems' basic currency is image rather than argument, but the images work together to convey a broadly coherent, if necessarily imprecise, view of the world.

Necessarily imprecise, I say, because Polley's interest lies primarily with the fluid, the ambiguous, the indeterminate. A four-line poem, 'Marsh', neatly encapsulates his vision:

> where the estuary thinks
> the same things as the sky;
>
> where cows appear cloudy
> and go down to the sunset to drink.

Viewed in isolation the poem seems slight, but the concept that it handles so deftly – the observer's disorientation in a world of blurred distinctions – is an important strand in the complex web of meaning established by the collection as a whole. The proverbially inconstant moon is an insistent presence – "a nothing lit up like a something" ('Dark Moon'), a "subtle silver highness" displaying a "face like melted tallow" ('Lunarian') or a disquieting watcher, staring down with its "faceful of dark and speechlessness" ('The Dark'). And the recurring images of water – running water "flexing in moonlight" ('Following the River') or still water effacing the reflections of successive observers from its dark surface ('Tarn') – offer further suggestions of the world's uncertainties and the quixotic folly of our attempts at definition. In 'A Book of Water', the emblematic book of the poem's title is illegible, its words "too quick to read".

The inadequacy of words to a shifting and ultimately ungraspable reality isn't necessarily a matter for despair. In the collection's title poem Polley takes a playful approach, insistently repeating a word whose all-purpose ubiquity progressively erodes our sense of its meaning:

> Change will not happen by havoc alone [...]
> As if I was a pencil and havoc kept me behind its ear [...]
> We're thinking about getting a havoc, but we know it's a big
>   responsibility.

Similar concerns inform 'Virus', in which repetition operates in conjunction with verbal slippage of a more random nature – "gerbil for tea-towel or horsemeat for colander" – to produce a radically questionable text: "we breathe easier now we can see what we say / in smoke, and all feel less gerbil".

The nonsense of that concluding line makes, paradoxically, excellent sense in the context of this searchingly intelligent collection. Over the past decade Polley has emerged as one of the most interesting and accomplished voices on the contemporary scene, and *The Havocs* is likely to reinforce his already considerable reputation.

Jem Poster is Emeritus Professor of Creative Writing, Aberystwyth University, and author of a collection of poetry (*Brought to Light*, Bloodaxe, 2001) and two novels (*Courting Shadows* and *Rifling Paradise*, Sceptre, 2002 and 2006).

New Eeks

IAN McMILLAN

Oli Hazzard, *Between Two Windows*, Carcanet, £9.95, ISBN 9781847771391;
Olivia McCannon, *Exactly My Own Length*, Carcanet, £9.95,
ISBN 9781906188047;
John McCullough, *The Frost Fairs*, Salt, £9.99, ISBN 9781844713981;
William Letford, *Bevel*, Carcanet, £9.95, ISBN 9781847771926.

I'm addicted to new work, to debut collections; I love the promise of them, the excitement of them, the way they step into the poetic fray without apology or nervousness and just stand there going "Come on then, come on, come on!"

Here are four superb and varied first books to keep me happy for a while. Oli Hazzard's *Between Two Windows* is awash with the visceral power of language and that complex dance between language and meaning. At his most adventurous, as in the prose-poem sequence 'Home Poems', he reminds me of John Ashbery or the Roy Fisher of the longer works: "They that catch the frightening of horses in their lipstuck mouths, that is essentially the ranking supervisor in this situation, that are designing a kind of you that cannot be forgotten or neglected, that live inside a set of shelled variations whose outer layer is barely [...]" and so on until the words pile higher and higher, and you submit to them and let them wash you all over. It's partly a game, of course, but Hazzard is very good at games. He's got mirror poems here, where the two halves of the work end and begin with the same line ("Said another way, maybe it could have happened") and palindromic poems that mine understanding and emotion from their letters and phrases: "Marge, let's send a sadness telegram" and "Amen, icy cinema", for instance. The games become more than games, become ways of getting to the heart of language's infinite potential. *Between Two Windows* makes me want to seize the possibilities of every day, and describe them and write about them and use them as stepping stones for philosophical enquiry, endlessly. "Loops at a spool", as Hazzard says.

Olivia McCannon's *Exactly My Own Length* deservedly won the Aldeburgh First Collection Prize; it's full of beautifully crafted poems built carefully from compassion and empathy, whether they're remembering (and half-imagining) an intimate past, "Into Number Three they poured / The past, the present and the future / Held in the space between four walls. // The past tied up in the deposit / The present in the sum paid out each week / The future in someone else's pocket" ('No. 3'), or detailing in heartbreaking stanzas the fading away of a parent: "I know you can hear and every day now / we are living through the horror / Of the one-sided conversation." ('Conversation'). In the best possible way this is a self-help book, a collection that underlines the role that the heightened language of poetry can play as we try to make sense of our changing lives. She writes "Each page so busy and thronging / We won't see the digits changing." ('Book of Hours'). Except we will, because McCannon has pointed those changes out to us.

John McCullough's another prize-winner; his collection *The Frost Fairs* won the Polari Prize and, although there's some Polari in the book ("my eek hovers / above Lady B's sink, bleach storming my scalp") the rest of the *The Frost Fairs*'s standard English seems to brim and fizz with the kind of glamour and music that Polari has in abundance. 'Eek' is Polari for face, by the way. But you knew that, didn't you?

In 'The Floating World' McCullough describes fossils of iguanodon and mammoth that "strive for attention, claw over hoof" and it seems to me that the lines and images in McCullough's fine poems strive for our attention, too, in a way that makes them work as hard as they possibly can for their inclusion. Here's a stanza, almost at random, from the opening of 'Seascape': "Scaling hills, we clump through heavy air. / A missing sun's tarnished light / tints the Downs with Lovat, smoke." How hard those lines work: *clump* rings with two meanings, *tint* has the unwritten hint standing right behind it and *Lovat* appears out of the blue, making you scurry to check you understood its meaning, that it's a "dusty blue-green colour" but also, with the capital L, the specific name given to a colour used in Scots Tweed. And now, because you've taken your time with the stanza and McCullough has taken his time with the stanza, the poem works. McCullough writes love poems, and poems of place and loss and the contemporary gay experience, pinning down feelings and taking snapshots with enviable ease: "March thaws the ocean / and I resume spinning pebbles into the shoal" ('Cold Fusion'), "What I need to know / is whether you ache to prise free // the ankle I've left loosely wrapped / in a sheet. Singlespeak is boring." ('Sleeping Hermaphrodite'). In the end, like *Countdown*, poetry is simply about the arrangement of vowels and consonants, but McCullough does it so very well.

William Letford's poems often come, like Fred Voss's and Geoff Hattersley's, from the world of manual labour, which is usually unexplored territory as far as a lot of contemporary poetry in concerned. Letford works as a roofer and in 'Waking for work in the winter', the opening poem in the book, he describes the sheer hard work of actually getting out of bed to face the day: "Even though the frost hasn't left the hard ground rutted by the wheels of tractors / Even though tail-lights clog the motorway / [...] Get up / Like the dog that hears a sound in the dark / Get up". Later in the collection, in a short and glittering prose piece, he tells us that he prefers winter, though ("In winter I fight fifteen battles / from my duvet to the front door, and win. So keep your tanned skin / give me frost on the fence wire, and January.") and there's a sense that the writing is equally hard-won despite its occasional casual demeanour. The poems can be brutal, as in 'Taking a headbutt'("blood-metal darkness and the taste of brass / the bell was rung / i know i went somewhere / because i had to come back") and tender, like 'Impact Theory' ("Moonlight / shows me the girl sleeping with her back toward me. She has the outlines of stars / tattooed onto her spine. Each one smaller until the void beneath the duvet / makes it difficult to see"). Letford's poems in Scots make you think of Tom Leonard, but I think there are echoes of George Mackay Brown's lists and careful phrase-placing here. Either way, Letford is very much his own man. Particularly in winter.

Four first collections. Four new voices. One happy reviewer.

Ian McMillan is a writer and broadcaster. He presents *The Verb* every Friday on Radio 3.

❧

Trend and Transmission

ANDREA HOLLAND

Katha Pollitt, *The Mind-Body Problem*, Seren, £8.99, ISBN 9781854115744;
Eduardo C. Corral, *Slow Lightning*, Yale University Press, £14,
ISBN 9780300178937;
Susan Wheeler, *Meme*, University of Iowa Press, $18, ISBN 9781609381271.

Beyond the trend for reportage, much American poetry continues to engage with language at its most instinctive and, often, dangerous. All three of these American poets refuse the status quo by presenting love and loss via distraction, idiom and variation. This can be exciting, though at moments (especially in *Meme*) the voice may be working rather hard to force the vernacular, as if the everyday can save us. This eagerness is less evident in *The Mind-Body Problem*, despite its self-conscious title; it is the most lyrical of the three and less intent on unpicking whatever conundrum the speaker faces.

In the possessive parts of speech we meet 'my' ("my mind" and "my body") but as Katha Pollitt knows, 'my' and 'mine' meets 'you' and 'yours' and therein lies the delight, and inevitably the 'problem'. Even the unlikely 'Lilacs in September' which have "broken out / unseasonably" after a hurricane, talk to passersby: "What will unleash / itself in you/ when your storm comes?" From the out-of-season blossom to the nurse "coming off her shift at the psychiatric ward/ nodding over the Post" ('Night Subway') there is fascination and considerable detail in each of Pollitt's observations. This is a loud, bright, alive arcade of poems, yet an arcade which we know is turned off at night; there are glimpses of melancholy amidst the amusement. Imaginative shifts in 'Visitors' take the idea of seeing the dead in the living (the power of resemblance) so the "dead appear / not, as you might imagine, / to startle us with fear, or guilt or grief / or the cold fact of our own mortality, / but just to take pleasure again in everyday life."

Lot's wife, a familiar character in the past thirty years of poetry, is given an unpredictable edge. Indeed the section 'After the Bible', offers characters we think we knew (Job, Martha, right through to the Tree of Knowledge itself) in new form or voice, the latter pleased to have been, "however briefly, / the center of attention" ('The Expulsion'). Pollitt turns these dusty Bible folk into twenty-first century performers; characters who talk with confidence and wit. In this collection Pollitt reminds us we are both alone and jostling in a crowd, and there are times when we "welcome the sight of even a wrong companion, / a troubled house, so long as it's well lit". This is the kind of comfort which *The Mind-Body Problem* both seeks and secures.

The introduction to Eduardo C. Corral's *Slow Lightning* remarks on the circularity in the first and last lines of the book, in the repeated notion of servitude (obedience, master), but another theme is established and returned to: the word "nourishment" in line one is framed by "I ate" in the last line. And these are hungry poems: the speaker is "spinning on a spit, split / in half" like a hog in 'Self Portrait with Tumbling and Lasso'; in another the "moles / on my body disappear [...] leaving me ravenous" ('To the Beastangel'). In 'Want', a father kills and tears apart a blue lizard: "shoved the guts and bones into his mouth" and this act is followed by "the first time I knelt for a man, my / lips pressed to his zipper, / I suffered such hunger."

The book is marked throughout by taste and touch, by the meeting of bodies in comfort and sex ("Once, in a grove/ of saguaro, at dusk [...] I woke/ with his thumb in my mouth") ('In Colorado My Father Scoured and Stacked Dishes'). The voice presented in these poems, at times radical in its expression, juxtaposes confidence and vulnerability, sensuality/pleasure and violence, or at least a rough touch. And so we find 'Acquired Immune Deficiency Syndrome' is a "'scarlet / snake wound / in [the] dark antlers of a deer'". But this threat is juxtaposed by "the honey smeared / on its hind leg" there to be tasted.

The form, too, challenges and yet invites in its refusal to settle down; lines are broken, willfully, in the middle or dropped down, rather than across the page. Perhaps these contrasts and subversions are less of a surprise when we consider how the poet's identity (as a gay man, as a Latino poet) suffuses the writing. It is informed by, yet never subject to, this identity; the 'labels' are a position which the voice in these poems both resists and embraces, through language which rocks our perceptions of this identity with: "Proverbs, blessings scratched into wood / The tar of my country better than the honey of others" ('Cayucos'). This is the magic, yet very real, world marked by slow lightning and offered for us to try, to taste for ourselves.

A speaker in Susan Wheeler's *Meme* declares "'*why not do everything*'" but this last remark is not a question. It is more of a warning, everything is on its way, beware oncoming traffic. And for the voice in most of these anxious urgent pieces, we "Enter alone, exit alone. / And then the smashed car". So this is a busy, precarious road.

All three sections of *Meme* are characterised by conflict and interruption; in the 'Maud' poems, a disembodied Mother admonishes and commands, all chat and chide, within a form which frames the idiomatic phrases around a more lyrical observation; the mother speaks first: "Last time I had a dickens of a job getting it loose and then there was just one measly piece left", then someone adds, "What drums behind her is the thump of the / backhoe striped by sun in the picture window...". Perhaps the voice of the daughter/poet, but straight away this poetic observation dissipates with the Mother's scold, "Well, if you'd hold it where I could see it!" ('Hot Sketch'). This contrast of voices is funny/sad but perhaps at times overdone. It is a contrast most marked in the 'Maud' poems, but the other sections also provide moments of lyrical insight pushed against a comment in the vernacular; a catch-phrase, a trend, a meme: "In the intimate turn, the beloved's breath, she's suddenly there. *Whore*". And, more consciously, "[...] when will a face appear / that cancels full th'other? / Or will there be no more for me / of anodyne palaver?"

Introjection and internalisation, whether parental, social or cultural, stalk the voices in these poems and it can make for uncomfortable reading at times. At others, it can shock with a moment of rare tenderness amongst the wrecked cars and loss.

Andrea Holland is a poet and tutor at UEA. She won the 2012 Norfolk Commission for Poetry and has a pamphlet from Smith/Doorstop.

ʒ

Bright Riot

CHLOE STOPA-HUNT

Helen Ivory and George Szirtes (eds.), *In Their Own Words: Contemporary Poets on Their Poetry*, Salt, £10.99, ISBN 9781907773211;
The Forward Book of Poetry 2013, Faber, £8.99, ISBN 9780571299010.

Contemporary poetry in the UK is conspicuously diverse and Carol Rumens – meditating on what she dubs "Brand Brit-Po" in her contribution to *In Their Own Words* – strikes a warning note by suggesting that "the variety may indicate [...] superficial splintering rather than a true diversity with strong individual roots". The thoughtful mapping that Helen Ivory and George Szirtes have undertaken should be a sizeable counterweight to such concerns, however. Harried by the financial pressures of devaluation by the state, and a technological arms race daily altering the available modes of publication, poets of all ages are vulnerable to anxiety, as the contributions illustrate. The appearance of *In Their Own Words*, therefore, is timely. Described by its editors as a "gathering of voices", this prose anthology offers no formulaic instructions, but rather a wealth of models for thinking better about contemporary poetry. Ivory and Szirtes have not restricted themselves to sampling the view from the heights: of the fifty-six contributors, though many are widely read and much awarded, several have published only one collection and a minority have yet to put out a full-length book.

Contributors were asked only to write a short piece of prose on the subject of their poetics, and this freedom has yielded a vibrant assemblage of anecdotes and essays. Few poets have tackled the theoretical side of 'poetics', preferring to talk through the genesis of their writing lives or to illustrate their poetic practice with examples and personally significant citations. Comical honesty (Luke Wright disarmingly recalls that he "started writing poems to show off") sits side-by-side with clear, quiet tenderness, as when Philip Gross describes the reconceptualised language that he learnt from his father's progressive aphasia. Mimi Khalvati and David Morley impart something of the delirious half-gain, half-loss of poetry that is not monolingual. In Khalvati's words:

> [...] my sense of yearning, desire, hiraeth, saudade, the extended Ah! that is the breath of the lyric. This Ah!, being out of time [...], having its home in language while longing for the wordless domain behind language, is why I feel the circumstances of my life have conspired to make me end up writing poems.

The anthology's introduction suggests that poetry "involves precision of touch without exhaustion of touch", and precise observation characterises the delicately-charted psychohistory of many contributions. Helen Mort describes the organic expansion of poems experienced while she's out on a run ("As the poem grows, I become increasingly terrified I'll forget it"), and Ross Sutherland belies the persistent idea of live poetry as unthoughtful when he recalls trying "to let the audience into [his] ignorance": to bring making poetry onto the stage rather than a pre-made poem.

In Their Own Words is a book for poets who want to understand other poets, who will sympathise with and chuckle over these tales of hard graft, habit, irrationality and ecstasy. Without denying the work of writing, there is a pervasive sense that many of the poets want to believe in the self-lives of poems. "I must stay vigilant yet passive, not too excited, not guiding, just attending," Andrew Greig explains, while Sarah Law outlines a similar approach: "This quality of attention is the simplest way of describing the poetic impulse – or my poetic impulse anyway". The critic and philosopher Simone Weil said that "attention is the rarest and purest form of generosity", and ultimately it is this generosity that recurs across the diverse accounts collected by *In Their Own Words*. Offering an unprecedented glimpse into the tenets, principles and actual practice of British poets, this anthology merits, in its turn, attentive reading.

In *The Forward Book of Poetry 2013*, the judges' eclecticism is everywhere manifest: on the shortlist for Best Collection, Geoffrey Hill's diamond-cut, compacted virtuosity is companioned by, among others, Beverley Bie Brahic's spacious and painterly poems of affect. Jorie Graham's *PLACE* secured the prize for Best Collection, and her poetic lens seems by turns irradiated and desolate, summoning the tragedy of a small child "already condemned to this one soul", or urging:

> [...] see it again – a yellow
> daisy, the sun
> strafing the petals once
> across, and the yellow which could be a god why not,

The shortlist for the Felix Dennis Prize for Best First Collection also demonstrates a spirit of critical open-mindedness, ranging as it does from Lucy Hamilton's luminous prose poems to the macabre repurposed balladry of Rhian Edwards's 'Girl Meats Boy'. Jacob Sam-La Rose unleashes an incantatory lyric realism in 'After Lazerdrome, McDonalds, Peckham Rye', while Loretta Collins Klobah's 'La Madonna Urbana' is a cantata of neomacaronic energy, weaving English with Spanish and aesthetic munificence with destitution. These first collections all seek in disparate ways to concretise, at once to capture and captivate the real, and Sam Riviere's *81 Austerities*, which carried off the prize, showcases the poetic potential of ludic hypermodernity performed through the medium of relentlessly impish textuality.

The Commended poems, and in particular those shortlisted for the Forward Prize for Best Single Poem, form a glittering motley of images, histories and lives. The poems are sometimes sceptical – "It was unclear to me whether literature could offer any salvation," Jane Yeh wryly observes in 'Yesterday' – and often lyrical, but the anthology doesn't shy away from British poetry's perennial involvement with elegy. James Fenton's memorial to Mick Imlah emerges from both 'Ode on a Grecian Urn' and D.H. Lawrence's 'Giorno dei Morti', yet its compressed form feels personal and particularised, while the aching restraint of 'Marigolds, 1960' (by Michael Longley) shows how occlusions can reveal almost more than is bearable. Denise Riley's 'A Part Song' (which won the prize for Best Single Poem) elegises a dead son and in doing so stretches poetry's ventriloquist capacities to an instrumentalised extreme, where aesthetic achievement can never be uncoupled from the failure of all poetics to enact literal recuperation of the dead. The elegists, observers and jongleurs in this anthology's textual *Wunderkammer* never form a united front, but they nevertheless remind us of the persistent boldness and reinvention of poetry in English: its unconformability, its bright riot.

Chloe Stopa-Hunt is a poet and critic from Cambridge.

The Anonymous Invitation

SPRING LAUNCH OF POETRY REVIEW AT KEATS HOUSE

Join our guest-editors Moniza Alvi and Esther Morgan, for readings by many of the contributors from this exciting issue

Thursday 18 April 2013, 7pm-8.30pm

Keats House
10 Keats Grove, Hampstead
London NW3 2RR
NEAREST TUBE: HAMPSTEAD OR BELSIZE PARK

Tickets are **free**, but must be reserved in advance: marketing@poetrysociety.org.uk or tel 020 7420 9886

THE POETRY SOCIETY www.poetrysociety.org.uk

The Anonymous Invitation

Cover: 'The Girl in the Wood' 2008 by Su Blackwell

Julian Fellowes   Jasper Fforde

The 33rd Winchester Writers' Conference, Festival and Bookfair 21-25 June, 2013

**The University of Winchester
With an In-depth Workshop
24-25 June 2013**

Join the feast of Masters' Courses, workshops, lectures and one-to-one appointments designed to help you harness your creative ideas and develop your professional practice.

For more information, visit our website
www.writersconference.co.uk
or contact Barbara Large MBE,
Winchester Writers' Conference,
University of Winchester,
Winchester, Hampshire SO22 4NR
Tel: 01962 827238
email: Barbara.Large@winchester.ac.uk

The **IRON** Age Festival
40 years of good books
1973 - 2013
15th - 19 May

Join IRON Press to celebrate four decades of publishing in Cullercoats. Readings, music, book fair, theatre, haiku boat trips, snooker tournament. New IRON book by DAVID ALMOND plus MELVYN BRAGG, IAN MCMILLAN, KATE FOX and many more, plus festival club

**T: 0191 251 6009
www.ironpress.co.uk**

NATIONAL POETRY COMPETITION 2012

❧

[...] harvest of dungarees scented by first fags,
notes in pockets to sweethearts; boots with laces undone.

– *Patricia McCarthy*

THE NATIONAL POETRY COMPETITION 2012

From more than thirteen thousand anonymous entries, Patricia McCarthy, Jane Draycott and John Freeman have been awarded the top spots in the National Poetry Competition 2012. Their winning poems and the seven commendations – by Edward Barker, Keith Chandler, Sally Goldsmith, Pascale Petit, Stuart Pickford, David Swann and Robert Stein – are revealed here in *Poetry Review*. Competition judges Vicki Feaver, W.N. Herbert and Nick Laird share comments below on each of the winners.

Vicki Feaver on Patricia McCarthy's 'Clothes that escaped the Great War'
"The surprising title of this poem was what struck us initially. But, as we read it, the whole poem grew on us more and more. We loved the journey it takes – both literally, as the horse and cart piled high with old work-clothes trundles down the lanes, and metaphorically, as these clothes come to represent the ghosts of all the young men lost in the Great War. It follows on from the wonderful poems written by poets like Owen and Sassoon about their war experience, to show the grief of the women who were left behind."

Nick Laird on Jane Draycott's 'Italy to Lord'
"We admired this dense, mysterious poem, which disclosed more and more as we reread it. It crept up on us; it moves from a London living room across the whole world, across cultures and myths and religions, through the encyclopaedia's "navigable miles", and comes down a hundred years later, into a strange new place where book-learning has been superseded by empirical experience, where the gold has all been "brought to light". The poem's quiet voice intrigued us, moved us, and finally amazed us."

W.N. Herbert on John Freeman's 'My Grandfather's Hat'
"From a gentle start in a domestic interior, this poem builds through careful observation to evoke a strong sense of lost time, and to embody the transition between generations, resulting in a sort of apotheosis of ordinary life through the simple action of an old man leaving a house. Both poem and figure move with an almost balletic grace, incorporating, in a single subtle movement, memories and past grandeurs into a walk down a garden path."

FIRST PRIZE

Patricia McCarthy
Clothes that escaped the Great War

Not the familiar ghosts: the shaggy dog of Thorne Waste
that appeared only to children, the chains clanking
from the Gyme seat, nor the black barge at Waterside.

These were the most scary, my mother recalled: clothes
piled high on the wobbly cart, their wearers gone.
Overalls caked in dung, shirts torn from the muscle strain

of heavy hemp sacks, socks matted with cow-cake
from yards nearby, and the old horse plodding, on the nod.
Its uneven gait never varied whether coming from farms

where lads were collected like milk churns, or going back
with its harvest of dungarees scented by first fags,
notes in pockets to sweethearts; boots with laces undone,

jerseys knitted – purl, plain – around coke fires.
And the plod, plod, quadruple time. Then the catch
in the plod from the clank of loose shoes, from windgalls

on the fetlocks of the horse, each missed beat on the lane
a missed beat in a heart. As a small girl she could see –
at their windows – the mothers pressing memories

too young for mothballs into lavender bags, staring out
propaganda posters, dreading the shouts of telegraph boys
from lines of defence and attack. As the harness creaked

and the faithful old horse clopped forward and back,
the lads were new-dressed in the years never to be had,
piled higher than high over the shafts of the buckling cart.

SECOND PRIZE

Jane Draycott
Italy to Lord

It's dark in here and forest green: *Britannica*,
sixteen oak trees in a London living room,
the little girl my mother in the bookcase glass.
Italy, Ithaca, Izmail, Japan, each page a mainsail
turning, HMS Discovery, *none of the rivers*
of southern Italy is of any great importance.

Like birds on long-haul flight, let not seas
or deserts, cliffs or icy mountain-tops
impede you. Jews, Kabir, Kabul, Kaffir,
from up here all seems clear (*all evil in the world's*
ascribed to Maya or illusion), then home at last
returned from all those navigable miles

to Lichen, Linnet, Logic, London, to find
a century has passed – the forest's cleared,
the animals all bared and scorched, the gold
all brought to light. I look into the glass,
discover there myself in dense shade, deep
and shadowy as on any wooded island.

THIRD PRIZE

John Freeman
My Grandfather's Hat

Most of the time I saw Granddad indoors,
first in his dark room with blue gas mantles
and a kitchen range and one tall window
in Poplar, then in the overheated lounge
of Aunt Nell and Uncle George's new flat
in Morden when he was in his nineties.
But he came to stay in our house sometimes,
and it must have been when he was leaving
that I saw him wearing his trilby hat.
It was grey and sleek like a new plush toy.
No one had ever made our two front steps
more like a staircase in a stately home,
not even Mum with her polio feet.
Crowning himself slowly, his own archbishop,
holding on to a handrail like a sceptre,
he turned with no more haste than one of the ships
he had sailed in round Cape Horn as a boy
in another century, approached each step
like a descent to be addressed with ropes.
Grandly he lowered one foot, then the other,
while we watched him, silently exclaiming
vivat, and the black and white chess-board
of the path to the front gate stretched out
like a long drive lined with waving flags.

COMMENDED

Keith Chandler

The Goldsmith's Apprentice

You will change into 'trashers', canvas shoes,
when you lock yourself in at eight.
Collecting your strongbox from the safe
it will be weighed. It will be weighed again
when you clock off at six.
You will sit at a vice with apron attached
to funnel the filed off dust.
You will blow your nose into newspaper
and not put grease in your hair.
Similarly, when you swill your hands
(your lunch box having been inspected)
it will be into this tank of sawdust
into which you will also expectorate.
All these – shoes, clothes, snot, sawdust –
will be burnt off at the end of the month
into a rough bar called an 'elmer'
worth more than you earn all year.

In return we will teach you to saw and buff;
to solder, blowpipe dangling from your lip
like a forgotten cheroot;
to cast by 'lost wax method'
rings and brooches, each mould unique
then melted out, weeping fat tears;
to hammer flake so fine
it will float like a feather above your face;
to draw out wire for filigree work
shinier than a girl's hair, stronger than her love;
to forge, clinging like slinky fingers
to Beauty's neck, chains so slim
no one but yourself may see the links.
You will breathe this atmosphere of dust
and soft percussion, dying at last
stoop backed, purblind,
your lungs lit up like a golden branch.

COMMENDED

Pascale Petit
Harpy Eagle Father

When I think of my father in the furnace –
the gas jets aimed at his chest,
fire-wings budding from his shoulders
and his mouth opening with its lit interior,
his tongue delicate as an icicle –

I want to be a harpy eagle mother,
feed dainties into his beak, its red
gape wide open to the Amazon.
I want to guard my precious snowflake
unsteady on his talons in the hot nest.

I want to guide my chick as he inches onto a branch
and shakes the blizzards of his wizard-wings.
Oh take your time, I want to say,
before the fledge. Perch here to watch
the howler monkeys of this forest.

Wait before you grow coverts
grey as ash, your primaries lifting
in violet air. Let the combustion chambers
of your under-wings pulse
with maelstroms of white down.

May the double haloes of your body
lift slowly and your head sprout
its adult harpy crest. Before
you're off, up and through
the trees, trailing a smoky wake.

COMMENDED
Edward Barker
The Mother Dough

He were forever glancing behind; I'd see him under streetlamps
as he waited for the clouds to catch up. When they did
from his pocket tin he'd bring out the mother-dough,

feverish with spoor-droppings, cuckoo spit, cobweb clots.
In those days he'd bet an owl from her feathers, a bride
from her ring, on a charm pluck the dimple off a hangman's cheek.

The night of the Ceilidh I wagered him for that sponge
of unusual properties; it was said how a lame mare had taken
the *Arc-de-Triomphe* after it was rubbed on her tendon,

how a tar-penny's worth could save a woman in still-birth.
His dice were no match, and he mulched into a dry, dead leaf.
I took for the heather with two of the dogs. One morsel

and the bitch gave birth on the spot. Them were rabid pups;
in seconds they suckled her to the bone. I drew lots with my shadow,
took the flake of it to my lips; rotten marrow, fermented sweetbreads,

enough to bring up the gag; that was when I heard my headstone ring
like St. David's bells on All Soul's Night, saw my bones
sprout from the grass in the tanner's yard, full of ghost·blossoms.

You can leave yourself alone only so long. To the false dawn
I was a pane of glass, the surface of a lake, either side of a hand,
but when I lifted it I saw there were no hands that were not wind,

no chambers in the heart but the clack of stones
they drop in the well of the pockets when they fit the noose.

COMMENDED

David Swann
The last days of the Lancashire boggarts

They were maybe on their last legs
even when Manchester first stuck its fingers
into the wound and began pulling out peasants.

Poor old monsters, who had clung
to their hosts' dark places! What a wrench
to see those hungry farmers ride away!

No wonder a few of them smuggled aboard
the carts – rode the moors to Salford and Ancoats.
I imagine them there, in that iron world,

those jealous creatures who had feared only horseshoes.
Who had survived the Norsemen's voyages,
the long centuries of rain.

Experts in growling, overturners of pails –
how did they cope, out-roared
by the looms, no livestock to lame?

Slowly they must have faded away, recalled only
in the folding of thumbs inside fingers,
the burning of nail-pairings and hair,

hoarded witcher marbles, crooked coins –
or come down to us as names: the Skryker,
Old Trash, Lubberfiends, Grindy Low.

Most of them were dead and gone by the time
I fell into the drizzle which had once
kept cotton soft. Manchester was old now,

its mills shushed. But you could still find
one or two of the old ghosts if you searched
the dark parts of the dead factories.

There, in those derelict places under the moor,
they roved their last stronghold, watching
as we went from our mothers to play.

COMMENDED

Sally Goldsmith
Thaw

A field snapped with frost and stitched with brittle docks,
a metal gate where I hung, still, like the horses there –

the grey standing gentle over the bay mare, held
inside their listening; wick-wick of a pigeon,

the chat of a jackdaw flock. Each second was a frozen bead,
but lovely to the touch. Once, he barely whisked his tail,

I watched. Then shifting my weight against the gate,
both turned and the mare lifted, nut-bright, out of her dream

then came slowly, and again on, slowly; the sky stretched
drum-skin, the sun low and sucked to a thin sweet.

She looked to the grey as if to say, *should I?* and a man
came, walking his dog. The mare whickered. *Grand!*

said the man. *It is*, I said, some strange thing thawing,
and she brought me her breath, timid to my hand.

COMMENDED

Stuart Pickford
Swimming with Jellyfish

For fun, the dolphins raced the prow,
flipping their white bellies over
for the crowd, some of whom ran

from one side to the other. Even
his wife smiled, gripping the rail.
After, she drove them up the coast

into a sea fret. Their flat's balcony
seemed suspended. She went for a rest.
On the beach, sun pressed to get through.

Families had parasols. Kids were netting
jellyfish. In a dinghy full of water,
they were pulsing like hearts, red

on yellow plastic. Happy to be stung,
he swam into coolness. His fingers flinched
as he brushed them but he pushed on.

Surely breaststroke would save him.
A jellyfish drifted through his arms, kissed
his cheek. He splashed as if his feet

were tangled but no one could see him.
The ocean felt darker feeding on
the pale mist. Trawling a wake behind,

he made the beach. The kids had vanished.
Jellyfish on sand, their buoyancy and gloss
a gritty blob. Too late to help them.

In the mirror, his face stared back.
Red cuts, raised like nettle stings,
tingling like with an electric shock.

His wife got antiseptic, plastered it over
but didn't ask why, resting her
fmgertips on the place he had been hurt.

COMMENDED

Robert Stein

Hommage de M. Erik Satie à Soi-Même

I am unaware I drink absinthe and drinking absinthe am unaware.
Suzanne has asked me what I am about, why I prefer furniture to music
and ham to any furniture.
My mother shook me awake every morning. So Suzanne, I say
it is the kind of love that is rhythmic, tender, surprising and hurtful.
'Suzanne I see you're leaving me' is scored for three pianos and a piece
       of ham.
Very fatty ham, endless white ham. It puts me in mind of clouds, of
       the white
close-prison-shaved skin my father had; his epaulettes; his sword.
       The white
hoods of the *Ordre de la Rose-Croix Canteloupe de Temple et du Graal*
which I am reputed to have founded.
Thank you for reputing that, Suzanne.

My last work I fear is this: *Relâche* or *Cancelled*.
My lungs, kidneys, heart, all is cancelled black on white.
In the *Pièce Imaginière (to be composed after my death),*
In the *Pièce Imaginière (to be drunk with a glass of white absinthe,*
       quickly)
the drums twirl and skirl like my father's moustache,
drill like that epée darting at me – ha!

In the air where the pieces I haven't written fall.
In the order of drunk, fallen-into-the-sea churches which
I will repute Claude has founded, in –

In the absence of absinthe I will drive the Citroën 45 times
around in circles as on *Relâche* the curtain falls.

I will write 7,000 pieces, some with my eyes shut,
out of the nonsense and noise skidding in my head;
ignoring the epée sticking out of my head;
after the pounding and *bruit* and Suzanne going in the white car.

And I will shake myself out of bed, shake you Suzanne,
shake everyone in the Bois du Boulogne out of
the ballet you've come for though I said it was cancelled,
out of whatever pyramid of people
you believe families are and out of rectangular dinner-tables

the kind of love that is tender in its absence, that is
sudden and iceberg-white, that is like being hit by snow
or finding the dinner-table gone and an orchestra there.

Going back to your lamp-lit home and the orchestra still there.
Ah Suzanne I do not understand it myself, so I will say it again.

CONTRIBUTORS

Patience Agbabi's versions of *The Canterbury Tales* will be published by Canongate in 2014. **Mona Arshi** has been selected for 'The Complete Works 2' development programme. **Alemu Tebeje Ayele** lives in London. **Mara Bergman**'s poems have been published widely in magazines. **Chris Beckett**'s latest collection is *Ethiopia Boy* (Carcanet/Oxford Poets, 2013). **D.M. Black**'s most recent collection is *Claiming Kindred* (Arc, 2011). **Judy Brown** is Poet in Residence at the Wordsworth Trust. *Loudness* (Seren) was shortlisted for the Forward and Aldeburgh first collection prizes. **Stuart Charlesworth** works as a nurse for people with learning difficulties. **Ned Denny**'s poems have appeared in magazines including *PN Review*. **Christina Dunhill**'s pamphlet collection was published by HappenStance in 2012. **Kit Fan** won the HKU Poetry Prize for his first book *Paper Scissors Stone*. **Rebecca Farmer** is an MPhil/PhD student in Creative Writing at Goldsmiths. **Jane Griffiths**' most recent book is *Terrestrial Variations* (Bloodaxe, 2012). **Selima Hill**'s *People Who Like Meatballs* (Bloodaxe, 2012), was shortlisted for the Costa and Forward poetry prizes. **Amaan Hyder** is a writer and lives in London. **Maria Jastrzębska**'s most recent collection is *At the Library of Memories* (Waterloo, 2013). **Petra Kamula** is currently based in Sydney. **David Morley**'s *The Gipsy and the Poet* is forthcoming from Carcanet. **Cheryl Moskowitz** won second prize in the International Hippocrates Prize for Poetry and Medicine (2011). *The Girl is Smiling* (Circle Time Press), was published in 2012. **John McCullough**'s *The Frost Fairs* (Salt) won the Polari First Book Prize and was a 'book of the year' in *The Independent*. **Gonzalo Melchor**'s translations and essays have appeared in *Poetry* and the *TLS*. **Zewdu Milikit** teaches in Gondar, Ethiopia. **Helen Oswald**'s *Learning Gravity* (Tall Lighthouse), was shortlisted for the 2010 Forward Prize for Best First Collection. **Katrina Porteous**'s long poems have been broadcast on BBC Radio, most recently, 'Horse'. **Sarah Roby**'s *This Afternoon and I* is forthcoming from Templar. **Valérie Rouzeau**'s *Vrouz* (La Table Ronde, 2012) won the Apollinaire Prize. **Carol Rumens**'s latest collection, *De Chirico's Threads* (Seren, 2010), consists of poems and a verse-play. **Anne Ryland**'s *The Unmothering Class* (Arrowhead), has been selected for New Writing North's Read Regional Campaign. **Mike Saunders** has an MA in Literature and Philosophy from the University of East Anglia. **Laura Scott** is completing her first pamphlet. **Bewketu Seyoum**'s pamphlet of translations is *In Search of Fat* (Flipped Eye, 2012). **Angus Sinclair**'s work is featured in the anthology *Dear World and Everyone in It: New Poetry in the UK* (Bloodaxe, 2013). **Julian Stannard** co-edited *The Palm Beach Effect: Reflections on Michael Hofmann* (CB Editions, 2013). **Marion Tracy**'s debut pamphlet is *Giant in the Doorway* (HappenStance). **Nicola Warwick**'s poems have appeared in magazines and competition anthologies. **John Wedgwood Clarke** is Leverhulme Poet in Residence at the Centre for Environmental and Marine Sciences, University of Hull. **Susan Wicks**'s translations of Valérie Rouzeau's *Pas Revoir* as *Cold Spring in Winter* (Arc, 2009) was shortlisted for the International Griffin Prize for Poetry and won the Scott-Moncrieff Prize. **Miranda Yates** lives and works in Stockport. **Heidi Williamson**'s *Electric Shadow* (Bloodaxe, 2011), a Poetry Book Society Recommendation, was shortlisted for the Seamus Heaney Centre Prize for Poetry.

LEDBURY POETRY FESTIVAL
POETRY COMPETITION 2013

JUDGE
Esther Morgan
CLOSING DATE
Tues. 9 July 2013

ADULTS
FIRST PRIZE £1000 and a week at Ty Newydd
(National Writers' Centre for Wales)
www.literaturewales.org/ty-newydd/

SECOND PRIZE £500 • THIRD PRIZE £250

See website for full details of Young People and Children's
competition section. Winners also have the opportunity to read
their poems at next year's Ledbury Poetry Festival (2014).

Entry fees: first poem £5, for each subsequent poem £3.
Children and Young People free for first poem.

**Go to www.poetry-festival.co.uk for details and to download
an entry form, or tel: 0845 458 1743 for a postal form.**

DATE FOR THE DIARY
LEDBURY POETRY FESTIVAL 5–14 JULY 2013
If you wish to join our email list and receive a programme
in May, please email: boxoffice@poetry-festival.com
www.poetry-festival.co.uk

LEDBURY
POETRY
FESTIVAL
2013

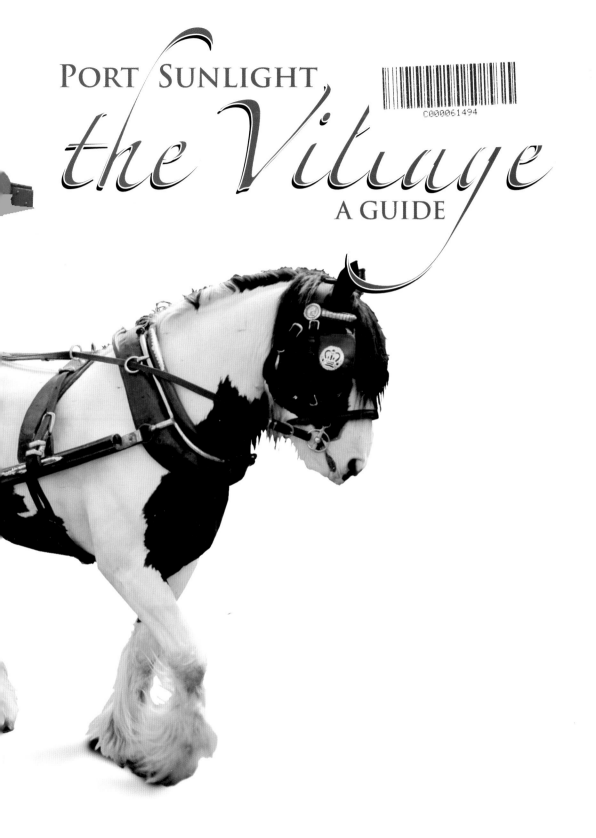

PORT SUNLIGHT
the Village
A GUIDE

MARGARET WILLIAMS

Port Sunlight Museum and Garden Village is a trademark of Port Sunlight Village Trust
www.portsunlightvillage.com

© Port Sunlight Village Trust and the authors
Published by Port Sunlight Village Trust
Designed by Val Evans Design
Printed by Tech Litho Ltd, Liverpool

ISBN 978-0-9559339-0-5

Port Sunlight Village Trust is a registered charity No 1074713

....

Front cover: A misty morning in the Diamond.

Contents

Foreword

You will find numerous guide books about Port Sunlight. They will extol the magnificent architectural heritage of the village, suggest walking tours and explain the development of the village from the first land purchases by William Hesketh Lever and his brother James Darcy Lever. This heritage is important and they significantly contribute to support the widely held belief that Port Sunlight is the finest surviving example of planned early settlement. We have chosen to give this guide book a different dimension by looking at the buildings through the people who lived here and who would have used them.

More than a century later, we are in danger of forgetting forever the people for whom this village was built and the customs and attitudes that they had. When we look at Port Sunlight we should always bear in mind some key facts including the sheer size of families in those early years where there were several thousand children living in the village, the very large number of clubs and societies many of which were housed within their own building. Even terminology in our daily language has changed so significantly that we have felt it necessary to include a glossary particularly for younger readers who will no doubt find some of the words used quite strange.

We have introduced characters into this book who are typical of people of the time, through them and the various aspects of social history that we cover in this book, we hope to give a richer glimpse of what life might have been like for a soap factory worker living in the village under the ever watchful eye of William Hesketh Lever.

It can be argued that Port Sunlight was one of the greatest social experiments of the late 19th and early 20th Century. Here there was free education up to the age of 12 and free further education beyond for those undertaking training for a trade or craft, free hospital treatment, living conditions in cottages that were a virtual utopia compared to anything else available for people on similar incomes and infant mortality at almost a half the rate in Liverpool. The blueprints of our modern welfare state were laid out here almost 50 years before.

The future of this wonderful village relies on future generations caring enough to ensure that it is appropriately conserved. We hope that you enjoy this book and the insights that it contains so that in some way it helps secure your support for this truly extraordinary place.

Lionel Bolland

....

Left: Spring Flowers

Port Sunlight's history

"This extraordinary man of vision provided a picture postcard home for his workers who, in return, worked hard and gave loyalty and affection."

The land on which Port Sunlight Village stands was purchased in 1887 by William Hesketh Lever. The successful soap maker needed a site to build his new factory and a village to house his workers. In total he bought 221 acres of land, with the village occupying 130 acres and his works taking up the remainder.

This extraordinary man of vision provided a picture postcard home for his workers who, in return, worked hard and gave loyalty and affection. From 1888, over 30 of the best architects in Britain designed the cottage houses which today number 900 dwellings. Beautiful open spaces, gardens and magnificent public buildings were also included in his plans. Keen to ensure good health for the workers, Lever provided doctors, dentists, opticians, midwives and in 1907 a cottage hospital.

Many clubs and societies abounded in the early days. Sporting activities, musical societies, literature, art and a variety of self improvement groups took place. Lever would frequently visit these clubs, taking with him articles collected on his world travels. The music group were often treated to hearing Mr Lever's gramophone which he had purchased in America and village children also received a sample of a new American treat – chewing gum.

....

Left: Bolton Road, c1914. The Employees Provident Society can be seen on the left.

Right: Sunrise over Dell Bridge, 2007

Lily, the canteen worker

"Hello, I'm Lily and I work in the Men's Dining Room at the Gladstone Hall".

"I have to be there quite early as the men drop off their mid day meal before they go into work. Mostly it's a billy can filled with stew or mutton broth, although some men do bring meat pies. My job is to make sure the food is piping hot for when the men return at lunch time and when I tell you there are eight hundred seats in the Hall you can see it's a big job.

There are also two dinner clubs for the male and female clerks, which have their own separate rooms. They have their own cook to make their meal but they do have to pay for the privilege. The Company supply all the crockery and coal for the range. Actually, there has been a bit of trouble lately over the crockery. All the village clubs which meet here in the evening have been using the cups and saucers and not replacing ones which get broken. The clerks are certainly not happy about that.

Anyway I must get on. All the tables and the floor have to be thoroughly scrubbed before the men come in to eat."

Both William and his wife, Elizabeth, had great fondness for children and were known as Aunty and Uncle Lever to all the little ones.

Each child received a book on their birthday, usually delivered to them by Mrs Lever herself. Every year a special 'treat' was held at Thornton Manor (Lever's country house). Horse drawn carts would collect all the children. Fairground rides, pony rides and boat trips around the manor lake were all provided. This was followed by tea on the lawn and at the end of the day each child was given a bag of sweets to take home.

In 1909 the rent for a kitchen cottage was 5s. or 6s.3d per week including rates. A parlour cottage cost 7s 6d, 8s.9d, or 10s. per week, including rates. The average wage for men in the factory was 25s. per week.

Talk of this wonderful village soon spread and in 1912 a musical comedy entitled 'The Sunshine Girl' based on Port Sunlight was staged at the Gaiety Theatre in London. This idyllic lifestyle continued until two great tragedies struck Lever and the village. In 1913, Elizabeth, Lever's beloved wife died, aged 63 from pneumonia. A heartache, from which, Lever never quite recovered.

In 1914 the village was plunged into war. Port Sunlight suffered such a terrible loss of men that at the end of the war it was virtually a village of widows and children. Post war Lever busied himself with the building of two of his greatest achievements, the magnificent Lady Lever Art Gallery, which

Hulme Hall, c1914. Crockery storage.

has often been described as the Taj Mahal of Wirral and the beautiful, poignant war memorial.

Lever died in 1925. During the post war years the village settled back into a tranquil life. The great depression of the 1930's was never far away but at least 'Sunlighters' had work and good homes. Trips to the local Thurstaston holiday camp could be arranged through the company. Dances were held regularly at Hulme Hall and once a year there was Founders Day which was held on the Sunday nearest his birth date (19th September) in memory of Lever. Held at the nearby Bebington Oval sports ground, it was a fun packed event with games and professional displays.

In 1939, war came upon the village again. This time not only the village people but the village landscape was to suffer. In total 34 houses were either damaged or destroyed by bombing. The village Co-operative store (which

The Gymnasium and open air swimming pool, c1912.

housed Macfisheries) was destroyed and the nearby bowling green damaged. Several villagers were killed during the raids. In 1947 a rebuilding programme had been implemented with all property, apart from the store, being replaced to the original design.

During the 1950's the village saw some prosperous days. Cars began to appear outside village houses, television aerials began to spring up. In the 1960's various renovation projects ensured that the village was fully up to modern living standards of the time. Gone were the days of the outside privy with houses converting a bedroom into a modern bathroom. Port Sunlight could certainly be classed as being part of the 'swinging sixties' with the Beatles making two appearances at Hulme Hall.

It was in the 1970's when a major change took place. People now wanted to be part of the property market. They wanted to own houses rather than rent them. By the late 1970's houses were offered to sitting tenants who wished to buy their home. Vacant houses were now placed on the open market. The long standing tradition of the firm providing the house, had come to an end. Immediately, people wanted to move into the village. They loved the green open spaces and the unique design of the houses.

Today the village is a thriving community. Clubs and societies again exist. The village school, Church Drive, provides all the latest modern facilities for education. Lever's beautiful Christ Church is a much sought after venue for weddings and christenings.

The Dell in bloom, 2007.

The landscape, with its rose gardens and green expanses, attracts thousands of visitors each year. Nearly one hundred and twenty years have passed since the village's inauguration. Times have changed, social attitudes have changed, two world wars have been fought and yet the charm and character of Port Sunlight have essentially remained the same.

William Hesketh Lever

"At sixteen William was a full time apprentice in his father's wholesale grocery shop (Lever & Co.), his first jobs being to cut soap bars and break sugar."

William Hesketh Lever was born on 19th September 1851 at No. 16, Wood Street, Bolton. William was the seventh child of James and Eliza Lever and their first and long awaited son. James Darcy Lever was born in 1854 and a further two daughters came along in the following years.

William was a happy and active child and at the age of six was sent to a small school for boys and girls which was run by the Misses Aspinwall. It was at this school that he was to meet two of the most important people in his life. A little girl called Elizabeth Ellen Hulme who was to be his wife and love of his life and Jonathan Simpson his lifelong friend. Jonathan became an architect and his son James Lomax Simpson (Lever's godson) was one of the thirty architects engaged to design Port Sunlight Village.

At sixteen William was a full time apprentice in his father's wholesale grocery shop, (Lever & Co.) his first jobs being to cut soap bars and break sugar. Later he transferred to the office and worked on the company books but William was eager to 'go on the road' believing the way forward was to get out and advertise your goods. Aged nineteen he became a traveller for the company and the business flourished. In 1872 James made his son a partner with a salary of £800 per year.

In 1874, now a successful businessman, William married Elizabeth Ellen Hulme, at St George's Road Congregational Church, Bolton. The newly married couple moved into No. 2, Park Street, Bolton and Elizabeth discovered what was to be one of her husband's hobbies throughout life, that of completely changing most of the appearance of any house they lived in. It was a happy life and for several years William carried on with much the same work as before. During the summer of 1877 an event happened that was to change their lives forever. William had been travelling on behalf of Lever and Co., and the business of the day being done decided to go home. However, on looking at his watch he realised it was only half past three. He turned his pony and trap and headed out of his usual territory towards Wigan. One order in Wigan lead to another and then another. As the orders increased so did the cash and before too long Lever & Co. had a new branch operating in Wigan, a new branch which William was completely in charge of running.

William Hesketh Lever by Philip de Laszlo, 1924.

By 1884 the Wigan office was firmly established and had even overtaken the sales of the Bolton office. William and Elizabeth travelled to the Western Highlands of Scotland for a well earned holiday. William was overawed by the scenery. He visited the Inner and Outer Hebrides and the town of Stornoway on the Island of Lewis. Here they were joined by his old friend Jonathan Simpson and William made the grand announcement that he was going to retire. Jonathan knew William better perhaps than William knew himself and declared later that he knew some new business activity was about to burst forth. Retirement would not suit William. William needed a new project to nurture and build now that the grocery business was such a success.

It was not long before the second announcement came. William was going to make soap, not just ordinary soap but special soap. Soap that would be distinctive and have a name that people would regard as a superior brand. On returning from Scotland he headed straight to a patent agent in Liverpool who provided him with a list of prospective names, none of which impressed him at the time. A few days later he was studying the list when a word flashed across his mind 'Sunlight'. He raced to the patent office and was delighted that nobody else had registered the name. Sunlight was his.

Port Sunlight Village

Strangely, James Lever was against his son's new venture, stating 'A cobbler should stick to his last'. However, he still agreed to loan his son £4000 and William withdrew from the grocery business to become a soap maker. With his brother James Darcy as his partner, (the now famous Lever Brothers and later the worldwide company of Unilever) William leased a factory in Warrington and the first consignment of Sunlight Soap went on sale in January 1886. The success of the soap was astounding, partly due to the product and partly due to William's clever marketing. It soon became apparent that the Warrington factory could not cope with demand and at the age of 36 William decided to look for a new site. On a visit to Cheshire with his friend William Owen (architect) William was struck by a piece of land on the banks of the Mersey River by the town of Birkenhead. It had all the requirements, transport facilities by rail and water, plenty of land and a good supply of local labour. Port Sunlight had been found.

On 3rd March 1888 Mrs Lever cut the first sod of the new development. Lever would have nothing but the best for his work force stating:-

'All tenement dwellings, flats and such like devices for crowding a maximum amount of humanity in a minimum amount of ground space are destructive of healthy life'

William employed over 30 architects to design the village and once work was underway the village rapidly took shape. As well as nearly 900 houses, William built a village hall (now the Gladstone Theatre), Hulme Hall girls dining room, a girls' institute, a men's social club, the Auditorium open-air theatre, the Bridge

Sam, the factory manager

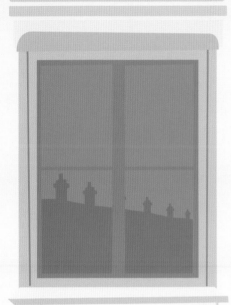

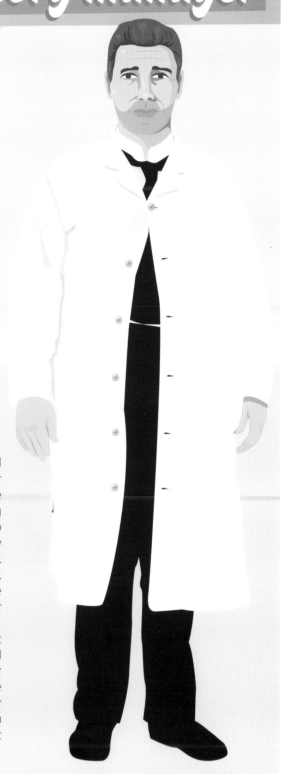

"Hello, I'm Sam, a manager in the factory. I started work as a post boy".

"Each day I would collect all the urgent mail from Port Sunlight, get on the train and deliver it to the Warrington factory. Then collect the Warrington mail, get on the train and bring it back to Port Sunlight. Later I transferred to the works and what struck me was just how friendly everyone was, including Lever himself. It was long hours, 6am to 6pm sometimes. Lever was always at his desk by 8.30am, he would ride all the way from Thornton Manor on his welsh cob.

Eventually, I joined the perfume department and became a foreman and later manager. I have travelled abroad many times, both for training and sourcing out new perfumes for the soaps. Lever always wanted the best no matter what distance it was to obtain it. I suppose you could say that working for Lever has brought me the sweet smell of success."

Inn temperance house but later a pub and the Lyceum village school. Later years saw Christ Church, a gymnasium and open-air swimming pool, cottage hospital, Technical Institute and the magnificent Lady Lever Art Gallery.

Over the next two and a half decades William Hesketh Lever became one of the worlds most successful businessmen. His works and village were visited by celebrities and royalty. In 1906 he was elected Liberal MP for Wirral, in 1911 Lever was made a Baronet, in 1917 Lever was made a Baron and in 1922 Baron Leverhulme was created a Viscount. His products became household names, Sunlight Soap, Vim, Lux, Omo and Lifebuoy to name just a few. Above all his legacy to the world, must be the beautiful village with its green open spaces, comfortable cottages and magnificent public buildings.

William Hesketh Lever died in May 1925 in his 74th year. The title Lord Leverhulme being passed to his only child William Hulme Lever. The world had lost a man of principal, a man of many talents, but most of all a man of vision.

Leverhulme Memorial

Viscount Leverhulme died in 1925 of severe pneumonia. This memorial to him, designed by Sir William Reid Dick and subscribed to by his colleagues, was unveiled in 1930.
The main figure on top of the monument represents Inspiration.
The figures at the base represent Industry, Education, Charity and Art.
All words associated with the great William Hesketh Lever.

William Hesketh Lever
Viscount Leverhulme
19 September 1851 – 7 May 1925

1851 – 19 September	William Hesketh Lever born, Bolton
1867	Entered father's wholesale grocery business, Bolton
1872	Taken into partnership in his father's business
1874 – 15 April	Married Elizabeth Hulme
1884	Decided to specialise in selling soap
1886	Started his soap works at Warrington
1888 – 3 March	Port Sunlight inaugurated
1888 – 25 March	William Hulme Lever, son and heir, born
1888 – September	Moved to Thornton Manor, Thornton Hough
1889 – 25 June	First boiling of soap at Port Sunlight
1895	Retirement of his brother, James Darcy Lever
1902 – 10 November	Made a Freeman of Bolton
1906 – 26 February	Elected Liberal MP for Wirral
1911 – 20 June	William Hesketh Lever made a Baronet
1913 – 25 July	Death of Lady Lever
1914 – 25 March	Visit to Port Sunlight of King George V and Queen Mary to lay foundation stone of Lady Lever Art Gallery
1915 – 1 July	Birth of Philip William Bryce Lever, grandson
1917 – 1918	High Sheriff of his native county of Lancashire
1917 – 4 June	Sir William Hesketh Lever made a Baron
1919	Mayor of Bolton
1922 – 11 November	Baron Leverhulme created Viscount
1922 – 16 December	Princess Beatrice opened Lady Lever Art Gallery
1925 – 7 May	Died at his residence 'The Hill' Hampstead in his 74th year

Principal Buildings

"A brief guide to some of the wonderful public building that William Hesketh Lever provided for his Port Sunlight community.."

Bridge Cottage

Designed by William Owen and built in 1894. Lever lived in the cottage at intervals during 1896 and 1897 while alterations were being made to his country house in Thornton Hough. Lever's son when writing his father's biography tells of his father's great interest in the social life of the village particularly during the early years of the village. He describes his father as a "good mixer" and encouraged other people to become good mixers too.

Lever could not tolerate class consciousness at whichever end of the scale. At a village social gathering he noticed people forming into 'cliques' he took the organisers to one side and made his thoughts clear. A village society was formed to organise events and gatherings to try and breakdown social barriers that might exist within the village. Bridge Cottage is the largest cottage in the village and the interior was featured in the film 'Chariots of Fire'. Today the cottage is owned by the Church.

Bridge Inn

Designed by Grayson and Ould the Bridge Inn opened in 1900. It took its name from Victoria Bridge which has now been demolished. At that time, the bridge carried the road outside over the tidal area of the River Mersey. The Bridge Inn was built as a temperance house until villagers demanded a vote for a licence. (Incidentally, the ladies of the village were included in the vote.) The licence was granted in 1903 after 80% of the poll voted in favour. Sunday remained 'dry' and this was the case until the late 1970's.

Just for interest, the price of a pint of beer in 1903 was a penny but this had risen to an astounding three pence a pint by 1914.

....

Left: Port Sunlight Buildings

Charles, the organist

"Hello, I'm Charles Morris the church organist and musical director for Port Sunlight".

"I work in the offices and I'm a close friend of Lever who loves music and art. I am also conductor to the Philharmonic Society and the Orchestral Society. Both societies are flourishing and give regular concerts with ticket prices starting at just one penny. Every summer Mr Lever holds a picnic in the grounds of Thornton Manor and sends horse drawn wagons to pick up the village choir who entertain his guests.

Of course, its not just music groups in the village, practically every taste and hobby is catered for. Football, swimming, cycling, to name just a few of the sports clubs. Then there are the self improvement groups such as the Scientific and Literary Society. We also have the Sick, Medical and Funeral Aid Society to help people in times of hardship. There's the Boys' Brigade for the lads and Girls' Club for the young ladies. At the last count there were twenty eight different clubs to join, nobody in this village could ever complain of having nothing to do."

Christ Church

Designed by William and Segar Owen from 1903 to 1904, Christ Church was funded personally by Lever in memory of his parents and given as a gift to the villagers. Constructed of red sandstone the united reform church holds 800 people and has a peal of eight bells. The very first wedding to take place in Christ Church was on 9th June, 1904 between Rhoda Butler and W.G. Dillon with the ceremony performed by the Reverend Sam Gamble-Walker.

When Lord Leverhulme died in 1925 his body was laid-in-state in the Lady Lever Art Gallery. Literally thousands of people gathered in the village to slowly file past the coffin. On Sunday 10th May a constant stream of people walked through the Gallery from ten in the morning until six in the evening. On Monday 11th May his funeral took place in Christ Church. The offices and factory closed and the whole village was in mourning. Lord Leverhulme and his beloved wife Elizabeth are buried in the narthex at the left hand side of the church.

Gladstone Hall

Designed by William Owen. Gladstone Hall was opened in 1891 by Rt Hon W.E. Gladstone and was used as a recreation hall and men's dining room until 1910. Lever was a lifelong Liberal and first stood for local election in 1892. He was defeated but eventually returned to Parliament in 1906 as Liberal MP for Wirral. Mr Lever frequently gave addresses at Gladstone Hall.

On the subject of the men's dining hall it is interesting to note the difference in the men's menu from the girls. The soup and bread option served to the girls is replaced by meat broth and bread for the men. Milk pudding or a tart for the girls sweet is replaced by boiled college pudding or rice pudding for men. Men could also drop off their own lunch first thing in the morning. This was quite often stew in a billycan which the canteen women would heat up at dinner time.

In 1910 the building was converted into a theatre and has remained so, although, cinema presentations have also been shown. In 2005 the interior of the building underwent extensive renovation with installation of new dressing rooms and bar area.

The Friends of The Gladstone Theatre is a volunteer group who work through all performances. This requires, three stewards, house manager, fire steward, three bar staff and two ice cream sellers. There are regular performances by The Port Sunlight Players and The Bebington Dramatic Society. The Theatre is administrated by the Gladstone Theatre Trust.

Hesketh Hall (The Technical Institute)

Built by J.J. Talbot in 1902 – 1903 the Technical Institute was paid for by Lever himself. A great believer in education, Lever's Technical Institute provided a wide curriculum for young people aged 14 to 18. Mathematics, languages and science subjects were taught alongside subjects such as wood-carving, cookery, dressmaking and sick nursing.

When the Institute first opened students were charged a small fee for classes. However, in 1908 it was decided that all 14 to 18 year olds should attend evening classes as a condition of employment and the Company then paid all costs. Regular examinations were held and certificates given by the Lancashire and Cheshire Union of Technical Institutes. In more recent years the building has been the home of the Port Sunlight British Legion.

Hulme Hall

Hulme Hall on Bolton Road, was built in 1901/1902 by the architects William and Segar Owen. Named after Lever's wife Elizabeth Ellen Hulme it was originally used as the Girls' Dining Hall, seating 1,500 girls at any one time. A typical meal would be a hot dinner, consisting of meat, potatoes and vegetables, followed by a fruit tart and cup of tea. This would have cost three pence halfpenny. (Approximately, £1.00 at 2005 prices)

Part of the Hall was used to house Lever's collections of furniture, china and pictures before the Art Gallery was built. Art lectures and classical music concerts were regularly given. In 1914, King George V and Queen Mary laid the Lady Lever Art Gallery foundation stone by remote control. They also paid an impromptu visit to a cottage in Bolton Road to see what a typical cottage looked like. Hulme Hall was used to home Belgian refugees during the early part of World War One (villagers donated over 100 clothing parcels) and later as a military hospital. In December 1918 the factory raised £70 to give the men 'a good English dinner' at Christmas. During World War Two the Hall was used as a centre for Dutch and Belgian refugees and later by the American Army. Wartime entertainment also took place with latter-day stars such as Tommy Handley, Arthur Askey, John McCormack and "Hutch" performing. The B.B.C. popular "Works Wonders" was broadcast from Hulme Hall several times during and after the war.

HULME HALL MENU 1909	
Dinner	2d.
(meat, potatoes, vegetables)	
Steak Pie	2d.
Milk Pudding	1d.
Boiled Pudding	1d.
Soup and Bread	1d.
Tea	½ d.
Tart	1d.
Bread and Butter	1d
(4 slices)	
Sandwiches	1d

Other visitors to the village from 1941 to 1945 included Billy Bennett, George Formby, Godfrey Winn and many military personnel. In 1962 The Beatles played at the Port Sunlight Horticultural Show dance in Hulme Hall. This was the first time Ringo Starr appeared with the Beatles, their fee was £30.

The Hall is now used for social occasions, exhibitions and conferences and was granted a licence for civil wedding ceremonies in September 2000.

Lady Lever and Fountain
'Sea Piece' by Charles Wheeler 1950

Presented to the village by the Trustees of the Lady Lever Art Gallery this magnificent sculpture was unveiled on Friday 28th July 1950. The striking fountain, in light green bronze represents a legendary seahorse with a triton and baby triton, on its back. Jets of water emit from the mouths of the tritons and also the dolphins at the base. Mythically Triton is the son of Poseidon and Amphitrite and lives with them in a golden palace in the depths of the sea. It was a dolphin which carried Amphitrite to Poseidon for the wedding.

The fountain was originally suggested by William Hesketh Lever, who felt that, the Lady Lever Art Gallery should commemorate the 100th anniversary of the birth of his wife, Elizabeth Ellen Hulme. Charles Wheeler, the designer, had the honour of switching on the fountain.

Lady Lever Gallery

Lady Lever died in 1913 and the gallery was given to the village by Lever in her memory. Designed by William and Segar Owen, it was opened by Princess Beatrice in 1922. It is a cruciform building in Classic Renaissance style with iconic porticos at each of the four ends and two great domes marking each end of 130 foot long main hall. It contains furniture, pottery, porcelain, sculpture, enamels, tapestry and needlework from Lever's personal collection. Two small figurines of a shepherd and shepherdess, which once adorned Lever's mantelpiece, at his first marital home in Bolton are displayed. It is claimed that Lever's amazing art collection began with these two small acquisitions. Leverhulme's son recalled that amongst his father's favourite paintings was a work by the artist John Singer Sargent, entitled "On His Holidays" However, on returning from an official dinner, his father told him that when he asked a gentleman at the table what he thought of the new Sargent at the gallery. The man replied 'I've not seen him yet, but it's good to give ex-servicemen jobs!'

In 1978 the building and collection were presented to Merseyside County

Council by Lord Leverhulme III. It is now administered by National Museums Liverpool. Lady Lever died 24th July 1913 before William Hesketh Lever became Baron (1917) and then Viscount (1922) Hence Lady Lever not Leverhulme.

Lever House

Designed by William Owen, Lever House opened in 1896 and proudly displays the Royal Coat of Arms on the front.

Lever House is particularly ornate inside with a beautiful mosaic floor depicting the Leverhulme Coat of Arms. Mr Lever and Mr James Lomax Simpson (architect) both had offices within the building. The original offices (most of which are still in existence) had high ceilings, wood panelled sides and doors and large coal fireplaces. Oak desks and Victorian paintings and pictures on the walls were the order of the day. Office boys ran messages whilst secretaries managed businessmen's diaries and appointments.

The factory was a hive of industry with packing departments, printing departments, woodbox making as well as soap production and bi-products such as glycerine. Accident prevention was paramount with the factory walls covered in signs such as 'It is better to be careful than be crippled' 'No smoking signs' and the use of chewing tobacco was prohibited. An anti-waste campaign ran and in 1917 a typical slogan was 'waste at anytime is a sin in wartime it is both a sin and a crime'

Lost Treasure - The Cottage Hospital

Designed by the architects Grayson and Ould in 1905 and officially opened in 1907 the Cottage Hospital was a miniature replica of an urban hospital. It originally housed only fourteen patients in twelve beds and two cots. Externally it was coloured light grey with rough-cast walls, casement windows with green shutters. Set on high ground surrounded by large open spaces with a large garden facing south. A spacious interior housed two wards (one male, one female), a surgery, waiting room, conservatory, staff room, nurses' dining room and kitchen, nurses' rooms and doctors' quarters. Staff comprised of a doctor, a matron, one staff nurse, two general nurses and three maids who were responsible for cleaning. Cleanliness was held in highest esteem. Baths were compulsory for all patients.

In 1930 the architect J.L. Simpson made considerable extensions to the hospital and over the coming years hundreds of patients were cared for. During the Second World War the hospital often acted as an A & E unit for casualties of bombings. Following the introduction of the National Health Service in 1948 the hospital was converted into a staff training centre. From 1984 until 2003 the building was used as a nursing home for the elderly. The building now houses the magnificent Leverhulme Hotel and Spa which opened in 2008.

Port Sunlight Museum

Designed by James Lomax Simpson, the architect featured within the Museum, the building was opened as a Girls' Club in 1913. James was the son of Jonathan Simpson who was the lifelong friend of William Hesketh Lever. Lomax Simpson was Lever's godson. James was an extremely talented architect and after several years working on freelance projects he was appointed Lever Brothers official architect in 1910.

The 'Girls' Club' was extremely popular, activities included dancing classes, dress making, knitting and wicker work. At the outbreak of World War One the women set to work on providing the men of Port Sunlight, who were leaving for the front, with warm clothing. The women even managed to obtain footballs to send to the men.

During the 1970's and 1980's the building was used as the Port Sunlight 'Residents Club'. Social evenings, wedding receptions and specialist functions were held. However, by the late 1990's attendance had fallen and closure became inevitable.

The concept of a new museum celebrating the vision of William Hesketh Lever and the life and times of his villagers came about during the early part of the new millennium. Port Sunlight Museum was over three years in the making and was supported by the National Lottery through the Heritage Lottery Fund and European Objective One for Merseyside. In September 2006, The Hon. Mrs Jane Heber-Percy, great granddaughter of the Founder officiated at the opening of the new attraction.

The Village School - The Lyceum

Built by Douglas and Fordham between 1894 and 1896, The Lyceum was the original village school. A school teacher's life was very different from today. Epidemics were common and schools would have to close for fumigation. The weather played a big part in school life with winter conditions quite often causing the school to close. The original school log books not only records the daily lives of the children but also the teachers and teaching assistants. Senior members of staff could write quite critical reports about junior teachers and school inspectors were often to be feared.

However the general impression from the log books is that of happy children and happy staff.

Church Drive School

Church Drive School replaced the Lyceum in 1903. However, the school had various ups and downs during its first year, as shown from the log book. Today, the school is run by the local education authority. Lord Leverhulme was always a regular visitor to the school, presenting prizes and awards and taking a keen interest in the children's lessons. I'm sure he would be amazed to see the children today. Every child wears a smart uniform of bottle green, grey and white. A new nursery section for pre-school children opened in 1989. The school also has its own internet web site to which the children have access. The sunken playground is a reminder that the building, now over 100 years old, stands on the edge of the main river channel, which ran through the village.

School Log

Good Times

15th August, 1903
The Coach Drives given by Mr Lever to the scholars were concluded today, all the children whose names are on the Register having had during the summer, a drive on the coach to Eastham.

Bad Times

September 23rd, 1903
School closed by order of the Medical Officer on account of a scarlet fever epidemic.

October 23rd, 1903
School re-opened on Monday. Attendance much lower during the week than before closing. This is due to the absence of children from infected houses, to the bad weather, and consequent ailments such as colds, croup, sore throats; and to the fact that some parents prefer not to run the risk of their children contracting the fever.

Sara, the schoolgirl

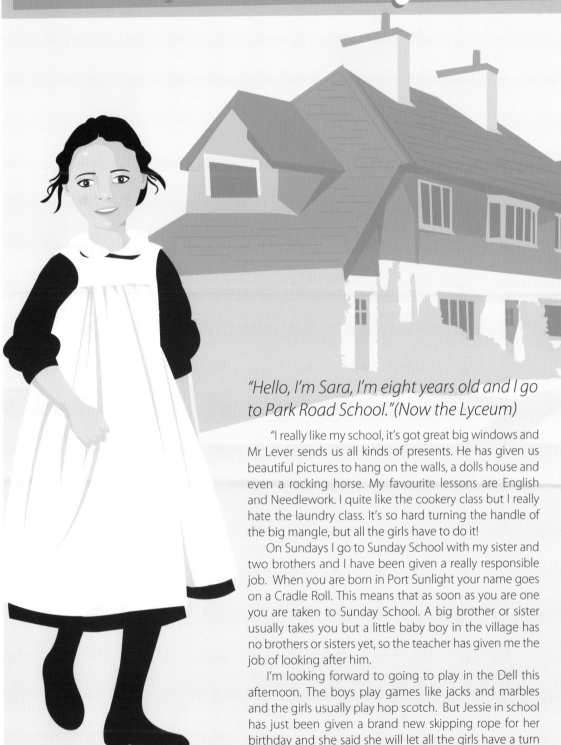

"Hello, I'm Sara, I'm eight years old and I go to Park Road School."(Now the Lyceum)

"I really like my school, it's got great big windows and Mr Lever sends us all kinds of presents. He has given us beautiful pictures to hang on the walls, a dolls house and even a rocking horse. My favourite lessons are English and Needlework. I quite like the cookery class but I really hate the laundry class. It's so hard turning the handle of the big mangle, but all the girls have to do it!

On Sundays I go to Sunday School with my sister and two brothers and I have been given a really responsible job. When you are born in Port Sunlight your name goes on a Cradle Roll. This means that as soon as you are one you are taken to Sunday School. A big brother or sister usually takes you but a little baby boy in the village has no brothers or sisters yet, so the teacher has given me the job of looking after him.

I'm looking forward to going to play in the Dell this afternoon. The boys play games like jacks and marbles and the girls usually play hop scotch. But Jessie in school has just been given a brand new skipping rope for her birthday and she said she will let all the girls have a turn of it."

POST CARD

SOUTHAMPTON

COMMUNICATION — PM —

My Darling Alice
Just a few words
here 8.0 oclock pushing
off to France Thursday
Shall soon be home Love
in very good health
keep your heart up

Mrs A Williams
21 Lower Rd
Port Sunlight
Cheshire

The War Years

"The Roll of Honour gives the names of 503 men who lost their lives and 4,069 soldiers, sailors and airmen who endured this terrible trial."

World War One

At 11pm on August 4th a state of war was declared by His Majesty's Government, between Britain and Germany. In September 1914 180 members of the Office Staff at Port Sunlight and at the Liver Buildings, Liverpool, were enrolled in one of the special battalions of the King's Liverpool Regiment, called for by Lord Derby, and familiarly spoken of as the 'Pals' Battalions, because they were intended to keep together men of the same city and as far as possible the same business and social interests.

In the same month a notice headed 'The Call to Arms' was put up in the Offices and the Works and Gladstone Hall was opened as a recruiting depot. By the end of the week a contingent of 700 men had volunteered. A Godspeed Service was held in the Auditorium on the Sunday afternoon.

Goscombe John's portrayal of women on Port Sunlight War Memorial.

Most of the men were sent to Salisbury Plain for training but upon arrival found that nothing was ready for them. The men needed 1,210 plates, knives, forks and spoons, which Lever Brothers readily supplied to them. When the weather turned nasty and the men wanted mackintoshes these were also provided. The women of Port Sunlight, sent constant supplies of warm gloves and socks. They also sent boxing gloves and footballs. Boxes of Aberdeen kippers were also sent out.

For the first time the women took over traditional male roles within the factory. Part of the factory was given over to shell production to keep the men at the front supplied. Ladies football teams were formed who played in charity matches to help the war fund.

One letter written by Private Herbert Stallard (Ambulance Corp) 1916 reported:

Shells rained amongst our poor lads and we stretcher-bearers never thought to see the light of day again. As two of my comrades were bringing one poor chap in, the fire became an inferno, and they rested under a tree. The wounded hero said 'Go away, lads, and get under cover. I'm wounded and it does not matter for me, but you can save yourselves.' Needless to say, our lads stuck to him and eventually got him to the dressing station.

The Golden Book, The Roll of Honour to Lever Brothers service men of World War One

Hulme Hall was firstly used as a refugee hostel and later into a full military hospital. Lever, provided rooms at Thornton Manor which were turned into a Red Cross hospital. The Port Sunlight Magazine 'Progess' reported monthly on the activities of the men with soldiers letters home, acts of bravery and tragic accounts of injury, illness and death.

On 11th November 1918 the 1st World War ended and the terrible toll on not only Port Sunlight but Lever Brother employees world wide was about to emerge. A publication entitled the 'Golden Book' was produced which contained the names of all Port Sunlight residents and Lever Brothers employees who had served in the Great War 1914 –1918.

The Roll of Honour gives the names of 503 men who lost their lives and 4,069 soldiers, sailors and airmen who endured this terrible trial. Loss of limbs, destruction of sight and undermined health from shell shock, trench fever, malaria, rheumatism, gas-poisoning and semi-starvation or ordeals suffered as prisoners of war had been endured by many of the surviving men. 512 men were wounded once, 91 twice, 20 three times and 6 four times. A copy of the book was presented to each serviceman or the surviving family. One copy of the book was laid beneath the Port Sunlight War Memorial and a copy is also kept at Christ Church.

THE GREAT WAR
Employee Awards and Decorations

V.C.	1
O.B.E. 1st, 2nd, and 3rd Class	2
D.S.O.	3
O.B.E. 4th and 5th Class	1
M.C.	21
D.F.C.	1
D.C.M.	11
D.S.M.	1
M.M.	52
M.S.M.	15
M.B.E.	1
Legion of Honour	1
Croix de Guerre	
Medaille Militaire	1
Medaille Maroc	
Gold Medal of St. George	1
St George's Cross	1
Mention in Despatches	
once	67
twice	5
three	1
four	2
Certificate of Bravery in the Field	1
Mention for National Service	4

Port Sunlight War Memorial

Lever commissioned his friend Sir William Goscombe John, to design the Port Sunlight War Memorial. The impressive sculpture stands 38 feet/11.5 metres from the ground and is 80 feet/24.3 meters in diameter. At the base of the cross are a group of soldiers symbolizing Defence of the Home. One soldier has a fixed bayonet another kneels firing a rifle, whilst a third is wounded and being helped by a nurse. A Boy Scout and women with children are also depicted. The four sections of the parapet depict Naval, Military, Anti-Aircraft and Red Cross Services.

War Memorial and Lady Lever Art Gallery.

The unveiling ceremony took place on the morning of 3rd December 1921. All the bronze figures were covered and as the crowd gathered the bells of Christ Church rang out. Lord Leverhulme had insisted that the actual unveiling should be carried out by ex-service men. A ballot was held amongst Port Sunlight's former comrades in arms and two names came forward, Sergeant T.G. Eames and Private Robert Cruickshank.

Sergeant George Eames

George Eames had worked in Number One Soapery at Port Sunlight prior to the war. A member of the 'Cheshires' he was wounded on 18th July 1916. George lost his sight, he had a finger shot off and shrapnel wounds to his left arm. On returning to Blighty, he was admitted to St Dunstan's hospital, where he trained for poultry farming. However, he became somewhat of a local celebrity performing at concerts as 'The Blind Baritone'.

Private Robert Edward Cruickshank V.C., London Regiment

Robert Cruickshank was employed by Lever Brothers, London. On 22nd June 1918, it was announced that he had been awarded the Victoria Cross for the following act of valour. The platoon to which he belonged came under very heavy fire and was forced down a steep bank into a wadi. Most of the men had been hit before reaching the bottom. The officer in command was shot dead, and the sergeant who then took command sent a runner back to Headquarters for help. The runner was killed as well as the sergeant. The only remaining N.C.O. asked for a volunteer to go for help. Cruickshank stepped forward. He rushed up the slope, but was hit and rolled back into the wadi. Climbing to his feet, he made a second attempt at the slope and was wounded again and rolled back. As soon as his wounds were dressed, he made a third attempt and was met by a hail of bullets. Badly wounded and unable to stand

Sergeant George Eames at the War Memorial unveiling ceremony.

he attempted to roll himself back but was left in a dangerous position. He lay all day with snipers shooting at him, one of which wounded him again. Throughout his ordeal, Cruickshank showed the utmost valour and endurance. Private Cruickshank had previously received two wounds in a victorious charge on enemy trenches in 1916.

Beneath the memorial lies a copy of the 'Golden Book' which contains the names of Lever Brothers employees who were in the Great War of 1914 to 1918. During this campaign a generation of young men were wiped out leaving a village of spinsters – women whose role in life would have been as the wife to one of those young men.

The Second World War saw two thousand men and women from Port Sunlight called up for service. In 1941 the village suffered at the hand of the Luftwaffe by night, several houses were badly damaged and five houses destroyed. After the war a further one hundred and eighteen names were added to the war memorial, eleven of which, were women.

The inscription reads:

THESE ARE NOT DEAD SUCH SPIRITS NEVER DIE

World War Two

On 3rd September, 1939, war was declared against Germany. His Majesty The King called for his people at home and overseas to stand calm, firm and united. These words were particularly true of the people of Port Sunlight Village. For many months the village had been preparing for the onslaught of another war. By September an Air Raid Precautions School was up and running and shelters were already in place. Auxiliary firemen were in training, classes in home nursing were available and village volunteers had dug trenches and filled sandbags.

Group Captain Guy Bolland CBE (decd) recalled in his memoirs *A life relived* that whilst he was serving as Squadron Leader at Hooton Airfield during the second world war, there was an unofficial trade agreement running whereby ammunition for the Home Guard was exchanged for soap from the factory.

Bomb damage, Port Sunlight.

As with the first war, the women of the village were eager to provide as much help as possible. By October the Women's War-time Sewing Parties group had been established. The Port Sunlight Library became an information depot where the women could enlist for sewing, knitting, or the making of such items as pin-cushions and lamp shades. These items were then sold on to provide much needed war funds.

By November, the Port Sunlight Allotment Holders' Society was in the process of being formed, an organisation which was to play a major part in the Dig for Victory campaign. As the war progressed large areas of the village were turned over to food production. The garden area from the Lady Lever Gallery to the War Memorial contained all kinds of vegetables.

The village magazine, Port Sunlight News, reported monthly on the village in war time and again published letters from the fighting forces. However, strict censorship was this time in force. Letters were simply headed "Somewhere in ...." No information of how the fighting was progressing was given, just that

Arthur, the home guard

"Hello, I'm Arthur Jones, but the lads in the Home Guard call me Digger because of my love for my allotment.".

"Well we all are encouraged to 'Dig For Victory'. I'm 61 years old and never thought I'd be back in uniform again after the last lot. Mind you with the government taking so long to get any kind of arms to us it's a good job that I still have my World War One infantry rifle. That was a bad time and my brother didn't make it back. He's listed on the War Memorial.

I'm in "E" Company of the 21st Cheshire Home Guard and us lads have reached such a high standard of proficiency that some recruits could transfer to Platoons. It's hard work though, I can spend all day working in the factory and then patrol the village all night. There is lots of 'undercover' work going on in the factory, ammunition, ration packs, even parts for planes and tanks, anything to help our men on the front. Of course there is still the soap and as I say to the wife, soap and water stop disease, so you might say it's also a form of defence."

the man was well and thank you notes for gifts. Slowly part of theses pages started to contain the Roll of Honour lists. No specific information on how or where the man had died, just that he had been killed in action and deep sympathy for his bereaved family.

In April, 1941, it was announced that the Local Defence Volunteers, recently rechristened The Home Guard, was now a fully organized military formation. After several months of training the men were ready to face any crisis that may arise with the same spirit and determination that had brought the Home Guard into existence. They were commanded by Lieutenant-Colonel Henry, who had a varied military career during the 1914-1918 conflict.

A Ladies Page contained all kinds of tips for women, from Make Do and Mend (turning old clothes into new ones) to coping with rations. Take a look at some of the ideas that were recommended in the summer of 1942:

Salad Cream
Now salad cream is unobtainable you can make a quite palatable salad cream by using unsweetened custard powder combined with salt, pepper and a teaspoon of vinegar. You can even use left-over custard the flavour is still quite good.

Gloves
Earn your best boy's – or somebody else's boy's gratitude, by stitching a strip of chamois leather inside the finger tips of the gloves you are knitting for the forces.

Starch
When your shopping trip is unrewarded, and the starch you are looking for is unavailable, try this. Place several peeled potatoes in cold water overnight. In the morning, when you remove the potatoes, you will find a sediment at the bottom which is pure starch.

A children's column encouraged 'every little boy and girl, who knows a brave soldier, to tell God his name, each night'

One thing the war did not stop was the village entertainment. Many famous personalities of the era visited Port Sunlight. Godfrey Winn (novelist and journalist), Billy Bennett (songs and comic recitations), Arthur Askey (comedian) and George Formby (singer and comedian) all entertained. Entertainment by the workers, for the workers was also popular. Amateur talent shows were held in the Girls' Dining Hall. In the later years of war regular dances were held at Hulme Hall. The village swimming baths (now the garden centre) were kept open.

But, by the end of the war, the actual foundations of the village were to pay the price of enemy action. Bombing raids destroyed five houses in Pool Bank, houses in Bridge Street, Church Drive and Boundary Road were also badly damaged. The Collegium, a large village store with meeting rooms above was completely destroyed. By 1951 the houses were restored to their former selves, but the Collegium was to be a lost treasure.

On 8th May 1945 (Victory in Europe Day), Hulme Hall was overflowing with revellers. Bunting adorned the village and huge bonfires burned. 1945 also brought the Port Sunlight War Exhibition, which showed just what had been really going on in the factory. Parts for guns, tanks, ships and planes had been produced. Periscopes and ration packs for the troops had all been secretly made. The Port Sunlight News of January 1946 was headed 'The Storm Passes'. It informed Port Sunlight that 'our united will to set things to rights will bring us towards the common goal of peace and security' and it did.

Digging for Victory in Port Sunlight

The Ministry of Agriculture's Drive for "Planning for Maximum Food Production" did not go unheeded in Port Sunlight Village. In 1939, when the need to "Dig for Victory" was realised, the Port Sunlight Allotment Holders' Society was formed, as previously stated. The movement arranged bulk purchases of seeds, fertilizers and lime for resale to members and gave free advice on the growing of crops and cultivation of land. In 1939, the Society had 200 members and this had grown to 400 in 1942.

The following crops were available to gardeners:
Beans (broad, dwarf and runner), beet, borecole or kale, broccoli, brussel sprouts, cabbages, carrots, cauliflower, celery, cucumbers, leeks, lettuce, onions, parsnips, peas, potatoes, radishes, spinach, savoys, shallots, tomatoes, turnips, and vegetable marrow.
Fruit and herbs were also planted.

Typical advice for the housewife (1940) for the week's main meal was:

Sunday	Meat (rationed), homemade stuffing, onion sauce, stewed fruit and custard
Monday	Soup, cold meat from Sunday, with salad.
Tuesday	Remainder of meat in hotpot served with beetroot.
Wednesday	Sheep's Head broth with mash followed by jam tart.
Thursday	Sheep's Head broth (remainder), with jacket potatoes.
Friday	Fish with mashed potatoes.
Saturday	Mixed grill (coupon dependent) served with mushroom and tomatoes.

Cottages Park Road

Living in the Village

"All tenement dwellings, flats and such like devices for crowding a maximum amount of humanity in a minimum amount of ground space are destructive of healthy life."

The Cottage Home

Lever deplored the cramped, overcrowded living conditions that were so prevalent in the Victorian era. Just across the Mersey in the city of Liverpool the greater part of the population lived in slums called 'Courts'. Terraced back to back rows, with little or no sanitation, where dirt and poverty lived side by side. In particular, Lever pitied the children. How, he asked, can a child who has never played in fields and knows nothing of the beauty of nature, but only seen the drunkenness and depravity of slum life, grow into a responsible citizen. He was determined that Port Sunlight would be a perfect setting to bring up a family. He wanted clean, healthy living conditions, well tended pretty gardens and wide green expanses for children to play on. To this end he employed over thirty different architects to design his vision.

Basically, two types of cottages were built. The kitchen cottage and the parlour cottage. The kitchen cottage comprised a kitchen, a scullery and a pantry, a downstairs bath with hot and cold running water and an outside toilet. The kitchen would have been the main family room. Upstairs were three bedrooms. Large families were brought up in these relatively small cottages, with girls in one bedroom, boys in another and mother and father in the third. The parlour cottage had a large living room (known as the parlour) a kitchen, scullery, pantry and a downstairs bath. Upstairs were four bedrooms. Outside the cottage it is hard to tell which are the larger ones as all have the same pleasant appearance.

For the time (1888) all cottages had the latest modern devices. In the scullery was a large copper for washing. The copper had a lid, so when not in use, it could be used as a table. Behind the scullery was a ventilated larder, which also had a sink with hot and cold water.

Miss Pearl, the postmistress

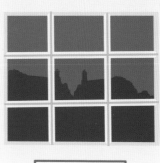

POST OFFICE

"Hello my dears, I'm Miss Pearl the postmistress".

"Now I came to Port Sunlight in 1894 when the small village shop became a Post Office. I am fully trained in Morse code so sending all the villagers' telegrams is no problem and I also operate the village telephone exchange. Although it has been rumoured that one of these new modern telephone boxes might be placed outside and painted bright red to match the post box.

It's a busy little place, the village gets lots of post and then there are the saving stamps, postal orders and the dog licences. I think half the village own dogs! Of course I must admit feeling very proud when it comes to the Old Age Pensions. Did you know that it was Mr Lever in his maiden speech to the House of Commons in 1906 who advocated Old Age Pensions?

All the villagers call into the post office, sometimes just for a chat. There are some folk who have said it's a 'gossip shop' well I know who she is and I could tell a tale or two about her."

With cold nights in mind, it had been decided that, the toilet should be no more than seven feet from the rear of the cottage. All the windows in the cottage were placed to give the best lighting conditions for the room and they all opened outwards.

Kitchens had an elaborate range and this was, sometimes, supplemented by a small gas cooker. Lots of cupboard space was provided both upstairs and down. A hat and coat rack was fitted by the front door. Every home had a gas supply, which was paid for by inserting coins into a meter. The sheer luxury of the cottages soon became renowned. The interiors of the cottages would have been immaculate, although overly ornate in the Victorian era. Cleanliness was ensured by one of the rules of tenancy, which gave a company representative the right to inspect the cottage interior at any time.

....

Employees Provident Society c1912.

Port Sunlight Shops

When Lever was building his village he was very aware of the importance of maintaining good relations with people of the neighbouring areas. With this in mind, he did not plan a large number of shops, but encouraged local tradesmen to bring their wares into the village. The milkman with his horse drawn wagon filled with milk churns would appear in the morning, maybe the coalman in the afternoon and various tinkers throughout the week.

However, in 1891 the first village shop was opened. This was a small store on the corner of Greendale Road and Park Road. By 1894 it had become the village Post Office, a gathering place for the villagers to collect post and packages and exchange all the local news and gossip. By the nineteen twenties it had acquired a public telephone box outside. When Lever was a Liberal MP he introduced a Private Members' Bill to provide state old age pensions payable to people through their local Post Office. This was adapted by David Lloyd George (Liberal Chancellor of the Exchequer later Prime Minister) in 1909 as part of his 'Peoples' Budget. Extremely picturesque, the building has been used in Post Office advertising campaigns but unfortunately became part of the small branch closure policy and ceased trading in 2005.

The Employees' Provident Society

Built in 1894 by the architects Douglas and Fordham, The Employees' Provident Society was simply known to the villagers as 'The Store', and run by employees along co-operative lines. The large ground floor of the building was were the villagers did most of their grocery buying. 'The Store' also provided a draper's shop providing dress making material and curtains, boot makers stall, ready to wear clothing, a butcher's shop, and a confectionary counter. A bakery and refreshment room where also in operation.

The upper floor housed The Girls' Institute or Collegium as it became known. A large room with white oak panelling and heavy oak beams. The walls were covered in pictures and the floor was polished boards. A large platform stood at one end of the room for use at meetings and lectures. Seating for 200 people was provided. The Mutual Improvement Society and The Boys' Brigade used the room regularly and several evening classes were held during the week. About once a month various clubs and societies held dances at the Collegium, with ample room for up to 50 couples. The cost was 3s. 6d per couple (about £11.00 today). The girls came in elegant dresses and men in evening wear.

Sadly, the building was destroyed by the bombing of the Second World War and never rebuilt. The church hall now stands on the site where the building stood just off Bolton Road and Bridge Street.

Trouble in Paradise

Of course, you can't please all the people all the time, as the old saying goes. The following letters were published in the Port Sunlight Monthly Journal, 1895. It is noticeable that both writers choose to remain anonymous.

Letter to the Editor (extract from a disgruntled villager)

Dear Sirs,

For a considerable time past the audience of the Sunday Evening Services at the Gladstone Hall have suffered a great discomfort and annoyance from the ill-advised conduct of a number of persons who appear to visit the service for the express object of preventing others from deriving any enjoyment or profit therefrom, if one is to judge from their deportment in the Hall on Sunday evenings. The grievance is no mere trifle, for the evil, I regret to say, is deep-rooted and comprehensive in its character. Loud conversation is carried on each succeeding Sunday almost uninterruptedly throughout the course of the service.

The incessant flow of buzzing conversation, the occasional laughter and the intermittent shuffling and marching of feet, the clanging of doors are elements sufficient to disturb the equanimity of an audience possessed of more than average nerves. The in-rush of cold air in wintry weather, consequent on the frequent opening of the door can scarcely be considered conducive to health. Trusting that the Hall Committee will see their way at an early date to devise means whereby the Sunday Evening Service may be conducted more decorously and in a manner that will be satisfactory to the audience who go there for pleasure or instruction, as well as the lecturer, or artistes who endeavour to impart these.

Yours Faithfully

MENTOR

Letter to the Editor (extracts from a letter in response to 'MENTOR')

Gentlemen,

The concluding letter of your interesting periodical, I support with the utmost personal enthusiasm. It is a question which I trust will be earnestly taken up by those in authority, so as to effect very speedily the restoration of peace, good behaviour and general respect amongst all and sundry attending the now famous Gladstone Hall.

And he's got his own grievance...!

I have a very uncomfortable and unpleasant grievance about our little model hamlet, and that is the continuous and well-nigh endless dog howling, which resembles the howling of ravenous wolves or yelping beagle hounds, disturbing our nocturnal repose, at the dead hour of night when our church yards yawn.

In addition to this we must not lose sight of another grievance. Notwithstanding the origin and history of cats, their seed and offspring are very alarmingly evident at Port Sunlight

Signed

SCOTIA

Port Sunlight today

"Since the 1980's Port Sunlight has achieved many prestigious awards for its landscape, being North West winner of Britain in Bloom on five occasions and voted the best village in Britain by the Britain in Bloom committee in 2001."

Port Sunlight became a conservation area in 1977. Nearly every building in the village is Grade II listed. Port Sunlight is arguably the finest surviving example of early urban planning in the United Kingdom. The village is almost completely   intact and has become one of the principal tourist destinations for Wirral. In the early 1980's Unilever began selling the cottages. Workers were offered their homes for sale and many, of course, took up the offer. By 1999 over 600 homes had been sold.

While this was going on, Unilever had also been seeking ways and means of handing the management of the village over to a suitable body so that the company could concentrate on its core business activities. After examining various models including the possible establishment of a housing association,

Left: Museum visitors enjoy a guided tour.

Above: Children dress up in Port Sunlight Museum.

association, it was eventually decided to create a registered charity and hence The Port Sunlight Village Trust was established in April 1999 - now using the trademark Port Sunlight Museum & Garden Village (PSM&GV). The whole of the village that remained unsold was transferred to PSM&GV which has been financially supported by Unilever. The long term aim for PSM&GV is to achieve a sufficiently high level of financial independence so that the future of the village is assured.

PSM&GV is managed by a Board of Trustees employing a small number of staff and a team of gardeners to carry out the various functions. Services for repairs and maintenance, architecture, building surveys and legal matters are procured from external firms and consultants as and when required. PSM&GV's charitable objectives are firstly to preserve and maintain the character and the land and buildings within the Conservation Area of Port Sunlight and secondly to promote understanding of the ideas underlying the foundation and development of the village. They also work with a number of village societies and resident groups.

> Each year Port Sunlight Museum & Garden Village plants 40,000 summer bedding plants, 107 hanging baskets and 40 tubs. During the winter months another 40,000 winter bedding plants and 20,000 spring flowering bulbs are planted.

PSM&GV has opted to retain its existing stock of houses rather than sell and this is a core feature of their business strategy. They own 253 tenanted dwellings along with 15 principal buildings that are leased to various operators or clubs. The Bridge Inn and Christ Church are the only principal buildings not in their ownership.

650 of the homes in Port Sunlight are privately owned due to Unilever's decision to sell houses in the 1980's. Almost all are Grade II Listed and therefore subject to planning controls covering everything from the style of the chimney pots to the colour of the front door. PSM&GV also enjoy the rights to restrictive covenants that apply to any of the houses that have been sold. Through these, PSM&GV can also contribute to the control of the village.

All the visible green space in the village is in the ownership of PSM&GV. No owner occupier owns a front garden. The management of the landscape and its maintenance to a uniform standard is one of the remarkable features of this village that distinguish it from almost all others. This invariably adds to the "theatre" of Port Sunlight and establishes a somewhat opulent presentation for the village. It does more than this however as it also unifies all of the buildings together into a setting quite unique and delightful to the eye. Residents are actively encouraged to maintain their rear gardens and house frontages with complimentary planting to a high standard and an annual Garden Competition is held to promote this.

PSM&GV also runs Port Sunlight Museum which is only two year old and forms the central platform to its mission of promoting the ideas surrounding the foundation of the village and its development. This was a £1million project funded by Heritage Lottery Fund and The European Regional Development Fund (Objective 1). Visitors are able to book walks with Village Guides who also give guided tours of the village to coach parties. The new learning facility in Port Sunlight Museum has just won the Sandford Award for Education.

....

A member of the gardening team.

Unilever Today

Port Sunlight is the base for the largest Unilever Home and Personal Care manufacturing site in Europe. Well known brands such as Persil, Comfort, Domestos and Surf are manufactured at Port Sunlight and Lever House is home to a number of Unilever's global and european specialist support functions.

In addition, Unilever Research and Development is located adjacent to the manufacturing site. This organisations drives the innovation of Unilever's Home and Personal Care range of hair, deodorants, oral, household and laundry global brands.

47

Acknowledgements and Glossary

Mrs Jane Heber-Percy* for archive photographs

Mrs Sharon Bolland, proof reader

Mr Lionel Bolland, colour photography

Ms Gina Couch, colour photography

Mr Gavin Hunter, archive photograph

The Lady Lever Art Gallery, reproduction of
De Lazslo portrait of William Hesketh Lever

Mr Jose Cardoso, colour photography

Mrs Elaine Hazlehurst, re Unilever

Gaynor and Ron Aston, archive photographs

Glossary

Billycan	A utensil for heating liquids on a fire
Cliques	A social group which restricts certain people from entrance
Croup	A viral infection which causes the lungs to swell Most likely to affect children between six months and six years old
Founders Day	A celebration held to commemorate the life of Lord Leverhulme held on the nearest Saturday to his birthday, 19th September
Gramophone	The first device for recording or replaying sound
Macfisheries	A fish and poultry market. Macfisheries had shops throughout the country and was acquired by Lever Brothers in 1922
Narthex	A separate porch or room usually located by the entrance of a church
Princess Beatrice	Fifth and youngest daughter of Queen Victoria
Privy	A toilet
St Dunstans	Opened in 1915, St Dunstans is a training centre for men blinded in battle
Sunlighters	Local term for people who live in Port Sunlight
Taj Mahal	A mausoleum located in Agra, India built by Mughal Shah Jahan in memory of his wife, Mumtaz Mahal
Temperance House	Alcohol free property
Trap	A small carriage which attaches to a pony

....

*Mrs Jane Heber-Percy, great-granddaughter of William Hesketh Lever is married to the
Hon. Algenon Heber-Percy and they live at Hodnet Hall, Shropshire, renowned for its
fine 60 acre gardens that are open to the public on selected days during the year.